HISTORY
STUDY KITS

-The-
Tudors

Structured Teaching Programme

Vital background information

★

Step-by-step lesson plans

★

Photocopiable reference sheets

★

Activity sheets

★

Assessment guidance

HISTORY
STUDY KITS

- The -
Tudors

Pat Hughes

Published by
Scholastic Publications Ltd
Villiers House
Clarendon Avenue
Leamington Spa
Warwickshire CV32 5PR

© *1994 Scholastic Publications Ltd.*

Editor
Helen Watts

Desk Editor
Lorna Gilbert

Sub Editor
Margaret Heeley

Series Designer
Joy White

Designers
Lucy Smith
Tracey Ramsey

Research
Andrew Brown

Illustrations
Jane Bottomley

Additional artwork by Roland Smith and
John Shipston.

Cover photographs
National Portrait Gallery: Elizabeth I. National
Maritime Museum: English and Spanish fleets
engaged. Christies Colour Library: Tudor coin.
National Trust Photographic Library: Little Moreton
Hall, Cheshire. Diary illustration: David Cuzik.

Excerpts from the History Non-Statutory Guidance
are reproduced by kind permission of the
National Curriculum Council.

The author would like to thank the following
for their help and co-operation:
Cynthia Gaskell-Brown, Plymouth Museums;
Janet Hollinshead, Liverpool Institute of
Higher Education; Hugh Waring and Phil Tweedie,
Liverpool LEA; Gill Goddard; The Mary
Rose Trust.

Designed using Aldus Pagemaker
Artwork by Studio Photoset, Leicester
Printed in Great Britain by Ebenezer
Baylis, Worcester

British Library Cataloguing-in-Publication Data
A catalogue record for this book is available from the British Library.

ISBN 0-590-53136-0

Teachers' notes

Contents

History teaching

The objectives of this Study Kit are:

● **To deliver the National Curriculum for history**
To help primary teachers to teach their children about the Tudors, in line with the requirements of the National Curriculum.

● **To aid classroom management**
The *Study Kit* is designed to be flexible and will complement most forms of school and classroom organisation.

Teachers can adapt and develop the materials to suit their particular teaching style and the needs of their children.

● **To explore both historical content and concepts**
Most children enjoy knowing facts and this *History Study Kit* is designed to give them considerable factual knowledge about life in the Tudor period.

This knowledge, together with the skills and understanding that they will develop through the activities in the kit, will help the children to appreciate important historical concepts such as the Tudor court and monarchy.

● **To develop children's historical skills and understanding**
Children need to know how historians work when they interpret the past and to be aware that there are specific historical skills that need to be developed, such as questioning and interpreting evidence.

History teaching must help pupils to adopt a questioning approach to life and to understand not only their own past but also the past of the communities around them.

This means that historical learning is on-going. Just as children continue to read and write after they have left school, they will continue to learn about the past.

The Study Kit comprises three elements:

● **Structured teaching programme**
This comprises:

● Teachers' notes which set the scene for teaching history in primary classrooms today; examine specific links between history and other areas of the National Curriculum; look at how the general requirements, as set out in the Statutory Orders, can be related to teaching about the Tudors; suggest relevant resources;

● Ten topic sections which contain Lesson plans to ensure that all aspects of the National Curriculum for history are covered, including recording and assessment, background notes and self-supporting activities designed to help children of varying abilities and ages to develop historical skills, concepts and understanding.

2 A collection of visual resources
This provides:

● The opportunity for children to use evidence for the period in the form of colourful and attractive primary and secondary source material;

● additional background material for '*Will's first battle*'.

3 'Will's first battle'
This is a children's text which:

● Provides a story context for learning about life in Tudor England;

● promotes imaginative thinking;

● develops an understanding of the use of historical sources.

Will's first battle

Additional copies of this children's book are available in packs of six at a reduced price of £19.99. Details are available from: Scholastic Publications Ltd, Westfield Road, Southam, Leamington Spa, Warwickshire CV33 0JH.

Children need to be introduced to history through a wide range of resources and perspectives.

National Curriculum history

The debate surrounding the publication of the *Final Orders* for history (March 1991) focused on the nature of history as a subject and the way in which it should be taught.

At Key Stage (KS)1, content was left fairly open but, at KS2, distinct content was set out in the form of Core Study Units (CSUs) and Supplementary Study Units (SSUs).

The *Final Orders* require teachers to use historical sources and recommend that children should be introduced to history from a variety of perspectives – political; economic; technological and scientific; social; religious and cultural and aesthetic.

The National Curriculum Council's *Non-statutory Guidance* for history provides planning grids so that content can be planned in a particular way.

Figure 1 on page 6 shows the grid for Tudor and Stuart times – Key Stage 2, CSU 2.

The headings on this grid require teachers to:
- Identify key issues and concepts;
- highlight particular content through which these could be taught;
- show the resources they intend to use as well as the teaching and learning methods;
- identify the attainment targets to be covered;
- show links with other areas of the curriculum.

This is a fairly prescriptive approach. The National Curriculum programme of study for KS1 is much more vague, so KS2 teachers must make a point of finding out the exact depth of the historical work that was carried out in the children's infant school or department.

Some schools will lay very solid foundations for KS2 while others may interpret the programme of study quite differently.

For example, the heavy emphasis on story in the KS1 programme could result in children entering the junior school with a strong background knowledge and understanding of some of the famous stories appearing in the KS2 Core Study Units. This can be strengthened and developed.

Other children may have had a very different selection of stories.

Initially, it was intended that the Core Study Units should be taught in chronological order. As this could present problems to schools with mixed aged classes, where children would struggle to keep pace with one another, it was later altered.

In the same way, this *Study Kit* has been designed so that teachers can mix and match the material to suit their pupils' age, knowledge and ability.

For example, children can read *'Will's first battle'* on their own, with their teacher, or the story can be read to them.

Figure 1

Title: Tudor and Stuart times   **Year: 5**   **Study Unit: Core Study Unit**

Focus: The way of life of people at all levels of society; well documented events and personalities

Key issues	Concepts	Content	Resources, Types of sources	Activities	Teaching and learning methods	ATs	Links with Other Subjects
How was Britain ruled? Was the character of the monarch important?	Monarch Government Nation	Tudor and Stuart rulers	Portraits of kings and queens Biographical details from sources Family tree Textbooks and library books	Pupils discuss portraits and what they can tell us about the character of kings and queens Story of Henry VIII's break with Rome	Teacher presentation Group work Group presentations Discussion of Henry VIII's character and the break with Rome	AT3 AT1(a) AT1(b)	Art English
How did the monarch rule, live and entertain?	Court Patron	The courts of Tudor and Stuart monarchs	Descriptions of Elizabeth I's visit to Kenilworth Plans of Elizabethan houses Elizabethan music, drama (Shakespeare) Art and craft materials	Investigations of court life Pupils make a wall display or enact an entertainment with music, food Visit, video	Pupil research Discussion Wall display	AT1(c) AT3	Art Music English
How did different types of people live in the reign of Elizabeth I?	Trade Industry	The way of life of different groups in town and country	Textbooks, library books Inventories, pictures, local buildings	Groups investigate lives of different people and present information to class Discussion of differences between life in Tudor times and the present day	Group work, research, model-making Fieldwork Class discussion	AT3 AT1(c)	Economic and Industrial Understanding, Art English Technology
What did people believe? Why was religion important?	Church Belief Persecution	Religious changes Religion in everyday life	Local church Pictures of churches and clergy in the reigns of Elizabeth I and James I Stories of the Gunpowder Plot	Visit to local church Look at pictures of clergy and churches, identify differences Story of hunted priest Pupils tell stories of Guy Fawkes, investigate whether story is true	Visit to church Comparison of pictures Story-telling Group discussion	AT1(a) AT1(c) AT2	RE (King James's Bible) English
What did people know about their own world?	Scientific discovery	Scientific ideas The Great Plague The Great Fire	Accounts of Plague and Fire Pepys' Diaries	What do we know about illnesses? Pupils study what people thought was the cause of the Plague Look at accounts of the Great Fire	Discussion Investigation of sources Role-play on whether to leave London during the Plague Newspapers about the Fire	AT1(c) AT1(b) AT3 AT1(c)	Science (gravity, Newton) IT
What did people know about the world beyond Britain?	Exploration Invasion Rivalry	The Armada Explorers The beginnings of the Empire	Maps, model-making equipment Computers/word processors Books, pictures, sources	Recap on 'Exploration and encounters' Pupils make models of galleons Receive information about progress of Armada and make decisions Pupils produce wall display	Teacher presentation Map work Decision-making Wall display	AT1(b) AT3	Geography English IT
Why was Charles I executed?	Parliament Law People	Civil War	Accounts of execution Books and pictures Tape recorders	Pupils study accounts of execution Research reasons for the death of the king Prepare 'radio broadcast'	Research Class discussion Radio broadcast or role-play Teacher presentation Story-telling about the Restoration	AT1(b) AT3	English

Cross-curricular links

English

Traditionally, English and history teaching have been closely related.

In the past, Her Majesty's Inspectorate (HMI) frequently criticised history lessons in junior schools for being little more than comprehension exercises in which children would be given a passage to read and were then asked questions to test their understanding of what they had read.

Certainly, history teaching should involve more than this but historical content can provide useful practice for language based skills, such as modelling, cloze procedure, mapping, comprehension and handwriting (see **Figure 2**).

The English attainment targets (ATs) and programmes of study will permeate any history lesson.

Historical content can be used to enhance listening and speaking skills and to improve reading and writing. For example, historical source material can be used to illustrate different writing genres. The diary in this *Study Kit* provides one model.

Alternatively, historical sources, such as the letters of Elizabeth and Mary, can be used to show purposes for writing. Children can also see how communications have changed with time.

The letters sent between overseas ambassadors, who worked in Elizabethan England, and their monarchs provide good source material for illustrating different points of view. They also show us how the great and famous looked and lived.

History also provides valuable information about the growth of language. Children can examine education in Tudor times and see the importance of Latin and its influence on words.

Ordinary written prose of the time is fairly difficult for primary children but church schools in particular may be able to use some examples with which the children are familiar, such as *The Book of Common Prayer* version of the *Psalms*.

Extracts from Shakespeare and Marlowe are also helpful when exploring the history of language.

Drama is seen as an essential part of the English curriculum and its uses in teaching history are well known.

Viv Wilson and Jayne Woodhouse, in their teachers' guide to *History Through Drama*[1], suggest that there are three key elements to explore:

1 A detailed investigation of a chosen period, based on available evidence, providing the context and framework for
2 The development of a personal history, through drama role-play, which is consistent with the historical evidence.
3 To complete the project, a day spent in role-play at an authentic site.

Delivering National Curriculum English through history teaching

AT1 – Speaking and listening

- Listening to the words of an historical story – autobiographical
- Noting particular genres – diary, journal, biography, narrative
- Discussing points raised in a story
- Drama and role-play
- Developing knowledge of the language of the day

AT 2 – Reading

- Reading a story
- Interpreting pictures and illustrations from a story
- Reading worksheets relating to tasks
- Historical tasks involving comprehension and understanding of a text
- Developing higher order reading skills through research and study activities

AT3 – Writing

- Personal writing – narrative, descriptive, creative
- Story writing based on different genre, for example, diaries.

Spelling

- Building historical word banks specific to: a particular period in history
- Practical use of a dictionary or computer spell-check

Handwriting

- General presentation of work
- Use of historical context for handwriting practice

Figure 2

The diary in this *Study Kit* provides all the material you need for drama work and it is possible to act out much of the diary in the classroom.

Children can work in small groups to dramatise the diary as it stands or expand and extend the story to incorporate new roles and settings.

Give the children Elizabethan names (see *How do we know?*, Activity sheet G) and, to be really authentic, help them with the language of the period so that they can use words such as *fie* and *forsooth*.

Art

The *Final Orders* for art recognise that, to obtain knowledge and understanding about art, craft and design, children at Key Stage 2 will need to know something about the history of art.

The Tudor period is ideal for examining portrait painting of the time and this will be discussed in greater detail later when portraits are examined as historical source material (see page 15).

Meanwhile, other techniques, such as brass-rubbing, can also be used to provide knowledge about historical source material.

Many parts of the country have commercially based brass-rubbing firms who will send representatives into schools and, for a small fee, children can rub brasses from different periods in the past.

Brass rubbings such as this one of Elizabeth I, from the Stratford-upon-Avon Brass Rubbing Centre, are not only fun for the children to do but are also excellent starting points for further investigation.

These firms usually provide good background information about the particular brasses they are using.

When examining other kinds of historical source material, such as buildings and sites, discussion about the original architecture can also involve aspects of the art curriculum and the influence of politics on art.

Technology

An understanding of any historical period will involve an insight into its technology. Domestic technology is one of the most obvious fields for research and practical activities in the primary classroom can include cookery, textile dyeing and weaving.

Jo Lawrie, in her book *Pot Luck*[2], provides several suggestions and English Heritage has a useful series of booklets on food and cooking[3], one of which covers Tudor Britain.

Children can also develop their information technology capability by using databases to record, display and interpret information they gather on the historical period. There are a number of relevant software packages available (see page 18 and Resources).

Mathematics

The links between maths and history are likely to be incidental.

Children exploring an historical building or site might be asked to measure part of it or they might be asked to identify various shapes in Tudor buildings and to practise working in different bases when looking at the currency of the period. English Heritage has produced a useful booklet called *Maths and the Historic Environment*[4], which is helpful here.

Geography

While it is difficult to relate a geographical topic directly to the Tudors, the geographical implications of the study units should not be missed.

Children should have access to maps that relate to the area and the time they are studying, such as the map included in this Study Kit showing Plymouth and its surrounding area at the time of the Armada. But if children are to understand their historical significance, they also need to be familiar with maps of the same areas today.

The two kinds of maps should be discussed together and the changes and similarities noted. It may help to enlarge these maps on a photocopier.

Learning about the Armada involves geographical understanding and skills. The politics of the event may be too complex for some junior children but examining the

A visit to an historical site or building, such as this Tudor farmhouse, helps children to understand more clearly how people in the past used to live.

growth of the Spanish Empire through maps can help to explain some of the political content.

The route of the Armada is particularly interesting and a map of this will enable children in other parts of the country to see the implications for their particular area.

The Scholastic *Starting History* pack on *Historical Maps*[5] provides more examples of this type of resource.

To study the voyages of discovery, which form an important part of the Elizabethan heritage, children need to have some knowledge of the world as known at the time.

Many junior children will find maps made at this time extremely difficult to follow so a simplified map should be used.

Children also need to understand the reasons for the voyages and this can be explained more easily through a visual resource, such as a map, than it can through the printed word.

Modern Ordnance Survey maps are useful because they show ruins, old settlements and roads.

Street names can also provide origin clues, although children need to be careful because there are several very modern 'Tudor Courts' in existence!

Tim Copeland's *Geography and the Historic Environment*[6] points out that almost every locality has physical evidence of how people in the past used to live and how they interacted with the place in which they lived.

It is this interaction between people and place which draws history and geography together into something that can be called the *historic environment*.

As children understand more about this relationship between people and place they can use their understanding to explore ways in which people in the past have changed the nature of the places in which they lived.

A visit to a small village such as Market Bosworth, near to the site of Henry VII's famous victory, shows how the buildings of the fifteenth and sixteenth century determined later settlement there. A village built today would look very different, both in terms of its road patterns and its housing.

The same is true of New Street in Plymouth, where Will's diary is set. It represents a particular form of historic town planning. In Plymouth this contrasts very strongly with the post-war building which took place. This is looked at in detail in the *Geography Study Kit* on Plymouth.

We know that the majority of people in Tudor times lived in the countryside, yet the houses in which they lived have long since disappeared.

The physical evidence of Tudor housing which remains tends to be house exteriors in market towns, such as Ludlow, manor houses, such as Little Moreton Hall in Cheshire, and the grander houses of the upper classes, such as Hardwick Hall in Derbyshire.

Today, many of these houses have been re-constructed to show what they were like in the Tudor period and from this it is possible to look at how they reflected the social organisation of the period as well as the type of materials used in their construction.

By the Tudor period, bricks were becoming fashionable building materials and were even used where the local material was stone.

Physical education
The requirements for dance in the PE programme of study can be related to dance in the Tudor era and a Lesson plan for Tudor dance is included in this kit (see the section on *Court life*).

Music
Music is seen as an important historical source and is looked at in greater detail later in these notes (see page 16).

However, to reach some understanding of music as an historical source, children need to develop their ability to *'listen to and appraise music, including knowledge of musical history...and a variety of other musical traditions'* (AT2 – Listening and appraising).

Examples provided in the Final Orders for music include listening to medieval dance music.

Science
Historical and scientific investigations have much in common. Children who have been encouraged from an early age to develop a questioning approach are more likely to become successful primary historians as well as scientists.

Science Attainment Target 1 requires children to look at scientific investigation, to ask *how* and *why* questions and to make careful observations. Clearly, these are cross-curricular skills that can be built on when children learn how to use historical sources.

There are particularly complex links between history and science in the study of the Tudor period.

Science, as we know it today, was virtually non-existent in Tudor times and it was not until the seventeenth century that the type of science illustrated in the other science attainment targets began – for example, the study of the movement of the stars and planets.

It is important that the children understand the reasons for this because they demonstrate the importance of scientific instruments and methodology. For example, scientific instruments that can be used to measure accurately, such as the microscope and telescope, were unknown to the Tudors.

Alchemy and astrology were really the only two areas in which any form of scientific methodology was used and these are both areas that are discredited by many members of the scientific community – although the interest in astrology among the general public is still strong.

Alchemy involved the futile search for a substance that could change base metals into gold. Two prominent Elizabethan alchemists were John Dee and Edward Kelly (**pictured here**) and it is likely that rich seafarers, such as Drake and Hawkins, would have helped to finance their work.

As leading seamen of the time, Francis Drake and John Hawkins would also have appreciated the usefulness of the stars as an aid to navigation. However, without telescopes there was little incentive for the development of astronomy. Generally, the Tudors were much more interested in astrology.

They believed that the position of the Moon and stars at the time of a person's birth determined their lives.

One of the few people who could have been described as a scientist by modern day criteria was one of Queen Elizabeth I's own doctors, William Gilbert.

He studied magnets and, in 1600, published a book called *On the Magnet*.

Because William Gilbert conducted experiments and drew conclusions from them, his methodology is broadly recognised as scientific.

John Dee

Direct links

The Final Orders for several core and foundation subjects involve historical content directly.

For example, the Orders for both art and music require children to become familiar with art and music from other periods of time, while some understanding of modern science and technology is required if they are to develop some perspective on the scientific and technological processes of a particular period in history.

In other subjects, such as English, history can provide a meaningful context for the delivery of a whole range of attainment targets and programmes of study.

It is important to recognise that history teaching means developing historical skills as well as knowledge.

History that is based solely on handwriting and comprehension activities may improve children's language ability but it fails to provide all the required historical elements of a study unit.

It is this focus on skills which has sometimes been absent from our history teaching in the past so that those children who have left school having enjoyed history have often found that their ability to become true historians later in life has been limited by the lack of some basic skills.

For this reason, the diary in this *Study Kit* comes with background information showing how the diary came to be written.

This should help the children to understand how historians work.

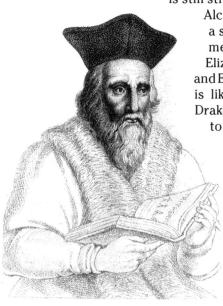

Edward Kelly

Cross-curricular issues

Circular number 6 (National Curriculum Council, 1989)[7] divides cross-curricular issues into three elements:

Dimensions, Skills and Themes.

Dimensions

Cross-curricular dimensions of race, gender and special needs must permeate the curriculum.

In the past, the provision for these dimensions has been particularly poor in the knowledge content of the history curriculum.

The History Working Party was keen to ensure that this was changed so that children could learn that history is not just about the rich and the successful but is concerned with everyone's past.

In studying the Tudor period, it is particularly important to recognise the presence and influence of women[8].

Elizabeth I is only the most obvious example. Others include Bess of Hardwick, Kate Ashley and, rather interestingly, Anne of Cleves who continued to live in England after her divorce from Henry VIII.

Race dimensions are much more sensitive. The gradual growth of the triangular slave trade between Africa, Britain and the West Indies, involved the transportation of vast numbers of Africans under the most appalling conditions.

It is not enough to know that John Hawkins was a famous sea captain.

His wealth was built on this triangular trade, as his crest clearly shows (see the section on *Life at sea*, Activity sheet B).

Older primary children should understand that slaves fought actively against what was happening to them.

Children can also discuss how, in Tudor times, any form of physical or mental disability was likely to bring people great suffering.

Disability frequently made it difficult or impossible for people to work and without work they starved.

Legislation during the mid-Tudor period had treated such poverty as a crime and punished it accordingly.

However, later, when the wars in England began to produce more and more soldiers with wounds and sicknesses who were also unable to find employment, some rethinking about poverty took place.

Poor people came to be seen as in need of help and, by the end of the sixteenth century, an early system of poor relief was established.

A distinction was made between the criminally poor and the deserving poor. The deserving poor were helped while the others continued to be treated as criminals.

The children can discuss these attitudes in the classroom and make comparisons with people's views today.

Do there appear to be greater divisions between rich and poor people in Tudor times than there are today?

Encourage the children to use a range of resources to find out about the lives of people in different social groups[9].

Bess of Hardwick was just one of many influential women in Tudor times.

Skills

Among the many cross-curricular skills discussed in **Circular 6** (NCC, 1989) are *'communication skills (oracy, literacy, numeracy, graphicacy), problem-solving and study skills'*.

History is an important medium through which these skills can be taught, setting them in a meaningful context.

For example, children can use many cross-curricular skills to develop their historical understanding by finding out more about life in an Elizabethan town at the time of the Armada.

Themes

The NCC identifies cross-curricular themes as

'elements that enrich the educational experience of pupils and include:

- *economic and industrial understanding*
- *careers education and guidance*
- *environmental education*
- *health education*
- *citizenship'*

NCC, 1989

Again, these can be set in an historical context. For example, a health education programme could look at provision for washing today and make comparisons with Tudor Britain (see *Rural life*, Activity sheet D), helping to explain the need for cleanliness today.

Meanwhile, economic and industrial understanding of the UK today could be aided by a background knowledge of the growth of industrialisation in Elizabethan England (see *Town life*) and the moral implications involved in the type of trading that took place between the Old World and the New World (see *Travel*).

Extracts from today's business news will show the children that such debates still have important parallels.

The National Curriculum Council guidelines on education for citizenship suggest that eight different components are involved.

They link three of these with the history that children at KS2 might be undertaking:

- Community;
- Being a citizen;
- Public services.

The history of the growth of any community is seen as more than just a localised event.

National and international links can be identified and some of these can be seen clearly in relation to the Tudor era.

Clothes, music, food, art and language were all strongly influenced by other countries.

In the portraits of the Tudor monarchs, furnishings and fabrics indicate the extent to which luxury goods were imported, and to which customs, such as the placing of carpets on floors, were being copied.

In the guidelines for teaching the component *Being a citizen,* the NCC suggests

that the study of early societies should include their laws and customs.

Examining the differences between past societies can provide reasons why wars were fought. For example, in Tudor times the long-running conflicts between England and Spain and England and Ireland.

The guidelines also suggest making comparisons between past and present in terms of public services and show how written and visual sources can be used here.

There are also other links which could be made with the components of citizenship, such as comparing work, employment and leisure now and then.

The NCC guidelines for environmental education link history with two of the seven recommended environmentally based topics. They suggest that the study of people and their communities should examine:

- Population patterns and changes; and
- How societies in the past have influenced, and been influenced by, their environments.

Another topic – Building, industrialisation and waste – can also have an historical element. The way in which an environment has changed over time has clear implications for the present.

The impact of changes in technology on communities can often be seen better by studying the distant past than by studying more recent history.

By looking at portraits, such as this one of Sir Walter Raleigh, children can discuss how some people came to own luxury fabrics such as silk and velvet.

The Welsh Orders for history state that pupils should learn about monarchs and personalities such as Edward VI.

Scotland, Wales and Northern Ireland

Scotland

This Study Kit links closely with the National Guidelines for Environmental Studies 5–14.

The Attainment Outcomes for Social Subjects include:

Understanding people in the past

which states that:

'attention should be given to placing the historical study approach appropriately within a chronological context; adopting methods of historical enquiry appropriate to the pupil and the context; using a variety of relevant sources of evidence; developing a knowledge of how people lived and understanding their social, economic, political and cultural developments, where possible illustrating the links between individual actions and major developments; and providing opportunities for pupils to interpret, identify with and respond to situations and events in a variety of ways.'

By the time the children have reached S2 they must have studied **Renaissance, Reformation and the Age of Discovery (1450-1700)** as part of their history work.

Wales

Life in Tudor and Stuart times is one of the compulsory history study units at Key Stage 2 in the Welsh Orders for history.

Pupils are required to study key issues and events in both Wales and England at this time and have to focus on the ways of life of people at all levels of society and on well documented events of the period. They should learn about:

- monarchs and personalities of the Tudor and Stuart periods;

- the Dissolution of the monasteries in Wales and England;

- the Bible in Welsh and English;

- sailors, pirates and explorers; the Armada;

- everyday life in Wales and Britain;

- housing and health;

- education and leisure in Wales and Britain.

From Key Stage 1, pupils should experience history using a wide range of sources, including artefacts and buildings, visual sources, songs, books and other written sources.

Northern Ireland

At Key Stage 1, children have to be introduced to a wide range of historical personalities and events related to local, national and world history.

They should gain experience of using a range of historical objects and visual material and should be given opportunities to develop their observation and investigative skills by exploring local evidence.

Key Stage 1 children should also use stories drawn from a variety of cultures and times to learn how to distinguish between real or imaginary people and events.

At Key Stage 2, the Tudors can be studied as part of the three school designed units (SDUs):

- **A study in depth**
involving the study of an aspect of history over a relatively short time – for example, explorations and encounters c1450-1550, or Elizabethan times.

- **A line of development**
involving the study of a theme over a much longer period – for example, ships through the ages; crafts in past societies; castles and fortifications; food and farming; sport and leisure; transport through the ages. Children should show links with local, national, European and world history where appropriate.

- **A local history study unit**
involving the investigation of an aspect of the history of the locality.

Historical sources

Primary and secondary

The programme of study for history at KS2 states that children should:

'*learn about the past from a range of historical sources including:*

- *documents and printed sources*
- *artefacts*
- *pictures and photographs*
- *music*
- *buildings and sites*
- *computer based materials'.*

Historical sources such as these may be:

primary – something that comes from the time that the historian is studying – for example, the portrait of Elizabeth I in the visual resource pack;

secondary – something that does not come from the time that the historian is studying – for example, Will's diary.

Interpreting sources

Teaching primary children about the Tudors involves the use of both primary and secondary sources but whereas the secondary sources, such as Will's diary, can be targeted directly at primary children, primary source material will need to be interpreted.

Sometimes this interpretation may take place outside the classroom – for example, by publishers in their decisions about what to include in their published material.

However, interpretations of historical sources should also take place in the classroom, where children are encouraged to develop their own skills in interpreting source material.

This is a key historical skill and the National Curriculum document sets out how this can be assessed in AT3.

Children can also examine different ways in which the past is presented to them.

For example, the children can discuss how, in Will's diary, the past has been interpreted by the author.

Guidelines on assessing these skills can be found in AT2.

Documents and printed sources

Written sources can take a variety of different forms.

The *Non-statutory Guidance for History* places them in six distinct categories – government records, local records, personal records, newspapers, literature and musical scores.

Such source material from the Tudor period is difficult for primary children, and indeed their teachers, to read.

Often, the writing is not clear, spellings and language have changed over the years and the sheer bulk of text means that written source material needs careful selection.

On Fact sheet C in the topic section on *Children*, you will find one way in which children can be introduced to an original text and can see how it looks when transcribed into something they can read.

But the advantage of presenting children with original written source material is that it conveys, much more clearly than a typed script, the need for careful interpretation.

Figure 3

Tudor text translation:

The 10th of July my little boys enter at table with John Fazakerley's wife and from that day until the 12th day day of August they continued all there. And then they played them at home 10 days. James and Robert went again and was sick and went again the eighth day of October.

↓

Who wrote this?

↓

For what purpose was it written?

↓

Why has it survived?

↓

What does it actually tell us?

↓

What inferences may we make from this?

↓

Do we have any other evidence that can be linked to this?

Where possible, use photographs of artefacts that are in context, such as these cooking implements in the kitchens at Hampton Court.

As **Figure 3** shows, questions are frequently raised for which there is no answer and understanding and accepting uncertainty about the past is an important stage in developing children's historical awareness.

Artefacts

Artefacts are objects made by people. They are non-written sources of evidence that exist in different forms, such as paintings, sculpture, pottery, tools, coins, carvings and remains of buildings. Much of the children's work here will involve looking at pictures. The visual resource pack and the diary with this *Study Kit* provide several examples.

The heavy dependence on photographic and illustrative material for this period has important implications.

It involves designing activities for the children that prevent their view of the past from being too flat and two-dimensional. Photographs have to be made to come off the page. Children need to be encouraged to use their imagination so that they can discuss what the objects would have been like to touch, feel and use.

Here, the help and support needed will vary according to children's understanding and whether the artefacts are set in a meaningful context. A single object behind glass in a museum involves a huge leap in imagination.

Where possible, the photographs of artefacts in this kit are shown in context, making the use of historical sources more interesting and relevant.

For example, the photograph of the Tudor kitchens at Hampton Court shows a large number of artefacts as they would have been at the time. Illustrations of artefacts are also important source material for primary children.

Artists use primary and secondary source material to ensure the accuracy of what they are doing but it is important to remember that they are involved in a re-creation of the past.

The illustration is their interpretation, and older children can use the work of different illustrators to show how interpretations of the past differ (AT2).

However, artefacts, like all other sources of historical evidence, are only partial representations of the past.

Work done in other areas of the curriculum, such as science and environmental studies, can help to complete the picture.

For example, the children can investigate the types of materials that are most likely to disintegrate so that they can see what is most likely to have survived from Tudor times – such as pottery, bones, ornaments, statues, furniture and coins.

Children should be taught to handle artefacts with care and answer the following kinds of questions:

- *What colour is it?*

- *What shape is it?*

- *What does it feel like?*

- *What is it made from?*

- *Is it a genuine Tudor artefact or one that has been made more recently? Give your reasons.*

- *What do you think it is?*

- *How was it used?*

Now draw a picture of the artefact.

Pictures and photographs

Tudor pictures and portraits are a particularly rich primary source and provide an excellent introduction to the period.

The National Portrait Gallery in London has postcards of all the Tudor monarchs and has portraits, such as that of Sir Henry Unton, which show the life of a typical Tudor gentleman and his family.

English Heritage's *Using Portraits*[11] is the most comprehensive guide for teachers although it is written for secondary teachers and needs modifying for use with primary children.

Fax-Pax[12] produces a set of 40 picture cards of kings and queens of England from the Norman Conquest to the present day.

Each card has a full-colour image of a monarch and has details of important events

Mary I, an example from the Fax Pax picture card sets (see Footnotes for details).

MARY I 1553 - 1558

Mary (b. 1516) was Henry VIII's eldest child. Her mother was Catherine of Aragon. She was distressed by the treatment of her mother and while Ann Boleyn was Queen she was kept at Ludlow and Hatfield, where she was brought up as a devout Catholic. She returned to court when Jane Seymour became Queen.

When her brother, Edward VI, died and Lady Jane Grey was declared his successor, Mary's followers persuaded the Privy Council to recast their support and proclaim her the rightful heir. She was taken to the Tower and Mary became Queen. The following year, after a Protestant rising, Mary judged that it was unwise to keep Jane alive so she was beheaded.

Mary restored the Catholic faith. She married Philip, heir to the Spanish crown. Parliament refused to accept him as England's King and the marriage was unsuccessful. Desiring a child to secure the Catholic succession, she blamed her bad fortune on heretics. As a result nearly three hundred Protestants were burned at the stake, earning her the nickname 'Bloody Mary'.

FAX-PAX

on the reverse side.

When looking at portraits like these, the children should have the opportunity to discuss the following types of questions:

- why portraits were painted in the first place;
- what kind of person was most likely to have their portrait painted;
- what they think the person in the portrait was like;
- how long ago the person in the portrait lived;
- what evidence the portrait can provide about life in the past;
- what evidence the portrait cannot provide.

Younger children can start by looking at portraits done today. Ideally, they should visit a gallery but it is also possible to buy postcards and work with these.

Children who are already aware of the symbolism involved in portraiture will have little difficulty in realising that Tudor portraits are full of messages.

Teachers of younger juniors may find it helpful to start with a photograph of Queen Elizabeth II, taken from a newspaper or magazine, then move on to a coronation portrait. The differences between photography and portraiture will become clear.

The children can then work on a postcard or picture of Elizabeth I, perhaps at her coronation, and note similarities and differences between the two queens.

Questioning can be open-ended – *What can you see?* – or more closed – *How many rings can you see?* – while recording findings can be done orally, in written form, or pictorially by copying.

Careful copying involves important observational skills and frequently children will raise other questions that occur to them while they are copying.

As one Year 4 child said about a picture of Elizabeth I: *Why does she look so white, is she a ghost?* Finding the answer to that question involves further research into make-up and fashions of the time.

Try asking the children to stand in the poses shown in the portrait. It soon becomes clear that the artists rarely copied every detail from real life.

Again, this raises questions about interpretation.

Few English monarchs have been as successful as Henry VIII in imposing their image on posterity and Elizabeth I continued and extended this type of portraiture.

Studying a collection of postcards of the same person will highlight the changes in the way people like Henry and Elizabeth were presented, showing their changing status and power.

Elizabeth even manages to avoid growing old in her portraits!

Portraits showing court life are important and accessible source material. They illustrate the different forms of clothing worn, the types of leisure activities pursued by the wealthy, and buildings, furniture and wall hangings.

However, children should also discuss the lack of pictorial information about the lives of other people living in Tudor England and they should realise that information taken from pictures is only partial evidence of the Tudor way of life.

Music

Music was something that both rich and poor people enjoyed in the Tudor period. May Day dancing and Morris dancing both took place in Tudor times.

However, the music would have sounded different because different instruments were used.

The lute was the most popular instrument, probably because it was a convenient size to carry. There are a number of portraits and miniatures of men, mainly young, using a lute to serenade their loved one.

Some stringed and wind instruments in use then are similar to those used today. The recorder was popular, as was the virginal – a keyboard instrument with strings that were plucked.

Many Tudor towns would have had paid bands to play in the street during festivals and celebrations while more wealthy Tudor families would often pay a small orchestra to play at meals and to give more elaborate performances on special occasions.

Inventories for such households frequently list a number of musical instruments.

Most educated people were able to read music so visitors and guests would be invited to join in the performance.

May Day dancing was popular in Tudor times and has remained so throughout history right up to present day.

Francis Drake had a small orchestra on the *Golden Hinde* on his voyage around the world.

The Tudor court and Royal Chapel were famous for music throughout the Tudor era, despite initial fears that Elizabeth would take a more puritanical view of church music. However, church music was simplified so that it was easier to understand the words.

Several companies have produced cassettes of Tudor music[10] and these can be used in different ways.

Some music is ideal for creating a mood for simple historical dramas. In one school, children listened to a few minutes of Tudor dance music, then discussed words which they thought described the music, such as posh, dignified, courtly and grand.

A visit to places like Speke Hall in Liverpool will complement any class project on the Tudors.

The children then practised an Elizabethan processional walk in which they dropped their heads and bowed and curtseyed before the monarch. No one played the role of the monarch – the idea was to create an atmosphere of her presence.

Later, the same children listened and danced to one of the four known Elizabethan dances.

Why not try this in your school, using the Lesson plan in the section on *Court Life*?

Buildings and sites

Although many Tudor buildings have survived, it is not always possible for every child to visit one. So, pictures and photographs may be the only way in which this particular source can be investigated.

Adults who have visited historical sites use their experience when they look at photographs of unfamiliar sites.

Children who have not had this experience depend on their teachers' interpretation. So, as with artefacts, children need to be encouraged to use their imagination if they are to learn how to interpret evidence from buildings and sites.

Usually, the survival of Tudor buildings has depended on stable ownership and, like home owners today, the occupants have repaired, replaced and added to the original structures.

Furniture has also been up-dated over the centuries and bathrooms, toilets, electricity, gas and heating have been introduced.

For example, some National Trust properties, such as Speke Hall near Liverpool, may have been built in the late fifteenth century but are essentially Victorian inside, so children need to be well prepared when studying or visiting such buildings and sites.

A comprehensive list of places to visit is given on pages 33–34.

Encourage the children to record any evidence of change as follows:

Evidence of change

Find four things that would not have been here in Tudor times.

1 _____

2 _____

3 _____

4 _____

Find four things that tell you that the building is old.

1 _____

2 _____

3 _____

4 _____

Find four places where the building has been repaired.

1 _____

2 _____

3 _____

4 _____

Where possible, try to organise some historical drama work on site. English Heritage organises many such events. Pictured below, children enjoy a day's historical drama at Helmsley Castle.

This helps to move the children's thoughts away from the architecture to exploration of life as it would have been in the buildings.

Computer-based materials

A requirement of all the programmes of study is that children develop IT capability.

Their ability to do this will depend on the availability of computers both at home and at school. When only one or two computers are available for use in a classroom this will direct the way in which they are used across the curriculum.

There are two main ways in which they can develop IT capability through a Tudor study unit:

● **the use of content-free software** such as word processing packages, desk-top publishing (DTP) and spreadsheets. Quite a few firms sell computerised pictures for DTP which will eventually have important implications for history teaching.

or

● **subject-specific software**. This is software which has been designed to cover the history study units. LEAs, software houses and publishing companies have been producing material on the Tudors for some time and the resources list suggests several different packages on page 32.

Organisations like English Heritage often arrange historical dramas on site, like this one at Helmsley Castle.

Planning

General considerations

Topics
This *Study Kit* has been divided into ten topic sections.

Each contains background information for the teacher on the particular topic area, a Lesson plan, photocopiable Fact sheets, Activity sheets, Research sheets and an Assessment sheet.

Display
A Tudor timeline is essential. This could be a published timeline, one that the teacher has created or one that the children have made.

The timeline shown here could be used as a starting point. More specific suggestions for display are provided with the Lesson plans.

Timing
The amount of time devoted to this teaching programme will obviously vary. So, the Lesson plans can be only a rough guide and teachers will need to adapt them for the children and in line with their school's planning objectives.

A total of ten hours is probably the minimum amount of time that could be spent on the Tudor part of National Curriculum CSU2, but each topic section in this kit provides ideas and practical activities for more than this. Provision has also been made for homework tasks.

Background information
This has been provided for each section to help teachers to stay more than one step ahead of the children. Teachers cannot be expected to be academic experts in every curriculum area!

Getting started
It is in the introduction of a new topic that the differences between individual teaching styles are most clearly seen.

Some teachers prefer the knowledge-based approach and either provide this themselves or ask the children to use reference books and other source material.

Other teachers prefer a skills-based approach and use resources to enable children to make their own discoveries.

The planning grid on pages 22–23 provides for a variety of introductory approaches.

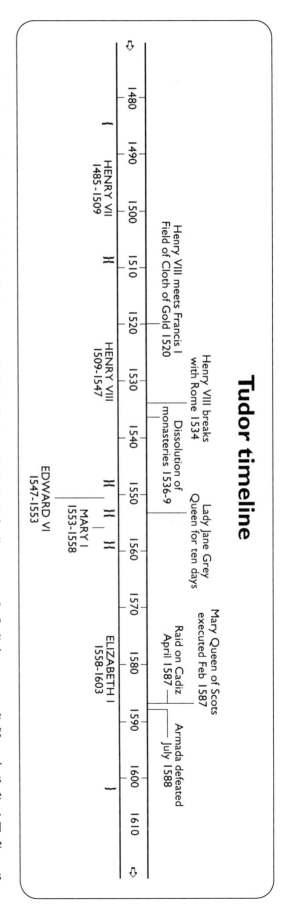

Tudor timeline

1480
1490 — HENRY VII 1485-1509
1500
1510 — Henry VIII meets Francis I Field of Cloth of Gold 1520
1520 — HENRY VIII 1509-1547
1530 — Henry VIII breaks with Rome 1534
1540 — Dissolution of monasteries 1536-9
EDWARD VI 1547-1553
1550 — Lady Jane Grey Queen for ten days — MARY I 1553-1558
1560
1570 — Mary Queen of Scots executed Feb 1587
1580 — ELIZABETH I 1558-1603 — Raid on Cadiz April 1587
1590 — Armada defeated July 1588
1600
1610

Planning grid

The grid on pages 22–23 is adapted from that for Tudor and Stuart times in the National Curriculum Council's non-statutory guidance for history (**Figure 1**) and provides for ten teaching sessions.

It enables the study unit to be taught through a wide variety of teaching styles although some of the sessions will require a whole class approach – for example, the lesson on Tudor dance.

Children can be encouraged to raise key questions through a brainstorming session in which they are asked to say what they know about the Tudors and what they would like to know.

Success depends considerably on the children's age range and ability and the amount of practice that they have had in raising questions.

However, as the National Curriculum document lays out what must be taught, teachers must ensure that the questions raised will cover what is required.

Brainstorming also helps teachers to find out what children already know about a topic.

Concepts

This section in the planning grid is essential as it ensures that work on the topic develops important historical concepts.

The concepts are taken from the 1985 HMI booklet on *History in the Primary and Secondary Years*[13].

This provides a list of 95 concepts and ideas which HMI found were commonly used in history teaching with pupils up to the age of 16.

These concepts are sometimes hidden within the National Curriculum programmes of study but often it is the level of concept development that differentiates children's ability in history.

The asterisk marks the content, resources and activities which will be seen at an earlier stage of a child's development.

For example, it highlights the kinds of activities that allow pupils with a low reading ability to demonstrate their understanding of particular historical concepts.

Content

The depth of content covered will vary according to children's age and ability.

The more detailed topic sections allow for differentiation of task as well as outcome. For example, content marked with an asterisk on the planning grid is particularly suitable for pupils whose historical concepts and understandings are limited.

Resources

In an ideal world, children would be provided with a wide range of experiences and resources, including visits to buildings, sites, museums and art galleries.

However, this is not always possible, so this section has been limited to what is likely to be available in most schools.

Activities, teaching and learning methods

This combines teacher-directed activities with free-standing activities.

The photocopiable sheets are intended to be free-standing, although children with reading difficulties will need support.

Recording and assessment

The final column provides an outline for recording and assessment in relation to the history attainment targets. Some topic sections are more detailed than others.

Listening to the children brainstorming ideas is one way of finding out how much they know and understand about a new topic.

Record sheet

To help you to record the children's historical skills and understanding, a record sheet is provided on page 36 which can be photocopied for each child and for each topic section.

Topic sections

This *Study Kit* features ten topics relating to the Tudors:

1 **The Monarchy**
2 **Court life**
3 **Town life**
4 **Rural life**
5 **Life at sea**
6 **Religion**
7 **Transport**
8 **Children**
9 **The Armada**
10 **How do we know?**

Each section is set out as follows:

a) Background information for the teacher
with black and white photographs and illustrations.

b) Lesson plan with:
   i   Objectives for classroom-based activities and homework
   ii   resources
   iii display
   iv   content – introduction, development, extensions, homework
   v   National Curriculum assessment.

c) Fact sheet(s) for the children

d) Photocopiable Activity sheets
Offering a range of activities, from drawing and writing to interpreting pictorial or written evidence.

e) Research sheets
These are included in some of the topic sections to allow the children to record information that they have found out.

f) Assessment sheet
This has been designed for the children to complete and allows the teacher to see clearly any gaps in the children's understanding. This can be used in conjunction with the Assessment panel on the Lesson plans.

The section on *Court life* includes an additional Lesson plan and two activity sheets for a Tudor dance session.

Lesson plans

Objectives for classroom based activities and homework

These indicate the particular historical knowledge, skills and understanding which the lesson is intended to promote in the children.

Historical skills are seen in terms of:

● chronology;
● using historical language and ideas;
● the use and analysis of evidence;
● asking historical questions.

Reference and information finding are included as essential cross-curricular skills, as is the ability to communicate basic ideas.

Display and resources
This section provides ideas for classroom display and for resourcing the suggested activities.

Lesson content
This offers introduction, development and extension activities for each topic area. However, how a lesson will end will depend on teaching style, so no formal endings are suggested.

Homework
Homework tasks with specific aims and objectives are included in most Lesson plans.

Sometimes they will follow on from work started in the lesson but often they will include a task that extends children's study skills and will therefore depend on children having access to reference books and somewhere to carry out the task.

For some children this may be difficult and teachers will have to find alternative ways to help them.

A sample homework sheet is provided in **Figure 4** on page 37.

Assessment
The assessment section on the planning grid shows which attainment targets are covered and indicates how teachers can assess children in terms of National Curriculum requirements.

However, this is intended only as a guideline and teachers should not feel that each lesson has to be an AT assessment exercise.

An asterisk is used to mark the skills, concepts or understanding that should be evident at an earlier stage of a child's development or which are appropriate for children with special needs.

Planning grid

Key questions	Concepts	Content	Resources	Activities, teaching and learning methods	National Curriculum assessment
Who were the Tudor kings and queens?	monarchy power authority chronology primary source evidence	Role of monarchy* Tudor family tree Key events	Drama props (for example, crown)* Pictures of Tudor monarchs Reference books	Drama – symbols of monarchy* Use of portraits as historical sources Tudor timeline Standing in portrait poses	AT 1 – 2c, 3c, 4c AT 2 – 1 AT 3 – 2, 5, 7
What was the court of Elizabeth I like?	monarchy evidence	Court life today and in Elizabethan times* Clothes, food leisure, music	Illustrations and portraits of Tudor court Reference books Photographs Tudor country house – internal and external	Discussion of duties of Queen today and in Tudor times Individual research on court themes Individual / group presentations	AT 1 – 2c, 4a, 4c AT 2 – 4 AT 3 – 1, 2, 3, 4, 5, 6
What was Tudor dance like?	evidence nobility monarchy	Music and dance in the Tudor court	Pictures of court dances Written source material Music of period	Learn the Pavane – simple / doubles steps Processional role-play	AT 1 – 3c, 5c AT 2 – 2 AT 3 – 1-4
What was life like in Tudor towns?	class continuity bias change economic law evidence	Way of life of people living in the towns	Will's diary Reference books Town maps Photographs of Tudor housing Illustrations Written source material	Use of pictures to find out about town life* Identifying bias in evidence Time capsule* Referencing and study skills	AT 1 – 2c, 3a, 3b, 4a, 4c AT 2 – 1, 2, 4 AT 3 – 1-6
How did ordinary people live in the country?	bias class change economics evidence	Domestic and farming patterns in Tudor countryside	Reference books Maps (country) Written sources – inventories surveys	General discussion on meaning of countryside Farming year Differences between town and country life	AT 1 – 3a, 3b, 4a, 4c, 5c AT 2 – 2, 4 AT 3 – 1, 2, 3, 4, 5, 6
What was life like for Tudor seamen?	colony cause change empire motive nation myth	Life at sea – merchant navy ordinary seamen explorers	Will's diary Illustrations and portraits Tudor ships Maps Portraits of explorers Reference books	Use of historical fiction to provide context for life at sea Reasons for exploring trade	AT 1 – 1a, 2b, 2c, 3b, 4a, 4b, 4c, 5a, 5c

Key Question	Key words	Content	Resources	Activities	Attainment Targets
What effects did changes in religion have on Tudor England?	Catholic, change, cause, evidence, Protestant, religion	Importance of religion in Tudor era, Comparisons between now and then, Multi-faith society, Priest holes, Mary Queen of Scots	Reference books, Bible, prayer book, Books of other faiths	Site visit to local church, Recording different religious centres, Tolerance and intolerance of beliefs	AT 1 – 2b, 2c, 3a, 3b, 3c, 4b, 5a, 5b, 5c; AT – 2-5; AT 3 – 1, 3, 4
How did people travel?	change, primary, secondary, chronology	Knowledge about different forms of transport in Tudor era	Illustrations and paintings showing different forms of transport, County maps, Reference books	Recording methods of travelling to school, Comparison of local area today with Tudor period, Different forms of transport today/Tudor times, Study skills	AT 1 – 2b, 2c, 3b, 4c, 5c, 6a; AT 2 – 1; AT 3 – 1-4
What was it like to be a child in Tudor England?	bias, change, continuity, evidence, class, cause, law	Changing nature of childhood, Childhood in Tudor period	Illustrations of Tudor school rooms, Will's diary, Reference books	Comparisons between schools and work then and now	AT 1 – 1b, 2b, 2c, 3b, 4a, 4c, 5c; AT 2 – 1, 3; AT 3 – 1, 2, 3, 4, 5
What was the Spanish Armada?	bias, Catholic, Protestant, Crusade, cause, evidence, motive, myth, propaganda, war	Events of the Spanish Armada and creation of historical myths	Will's diary, Reference books, Portraits, Maps, illustrations, Written sources, Computers	Current events – wars in the world today, Chinese Whispers game, Recording known events on a timeline, Newspaper reports from different points of view, Portraits as propaganda	AT 1 – 1a, 2b, 2c, 3b, 3c, 4b, 4c, 5b, 5c, 6b; AT 2 – 2-6; AT 3 – 1-6
How do we find out about Tudor England?	archaeology, bias, evidence, hypothesis	Writing about the past – fiction and fact	Will's diary, Reference books, Tape recorder, video, Computer	Re-reading of Will's diary and sequencing events in it, Identifying facts and fiction, Writing/recording different points of view, study skills	AT 1 – 1a, 2b, 2c, 3b, 3c, 4a, 4b, 4c, 6c; AT 2 – 1-6; AT 3 – 1-6

Using 'Will's first battle'

'Will's first battle' is a piece of historical fiction although aspects of it are fact.

Some of these facts are well known, based on evidence documented at the time – for example, the sighting of the Armada on 19 July 1588.

However, even this has to be treated with care as changes in the calender mean that dates are not directly transferable. The details about daily events in Will's life are based on more general evidence about life in Tudor times.

The author, Gill Goddard, has used this historical evidence to provide historically accurate information on features of Elizabethan daily life, such as the clothes Will wore, the food he ate and the type of work that he undertook.

The character of Will Martin, as described in the book, did not exist.

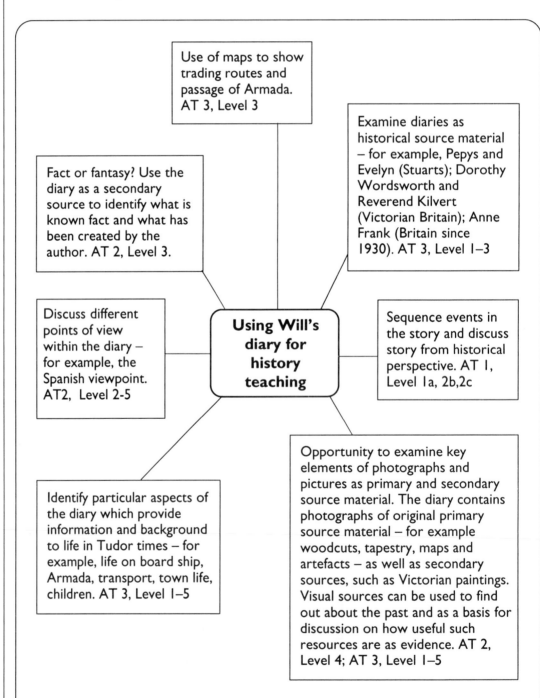

Use of maps to show trading routes and passage of Armada. AT 3, Level 3

Examine diaries as historical source material – for example, Pepys and Evelyn (Stuarts); Dorothy Wordsworth and Reverend Kilvert (Victorian Britain); Anne Frank (Britain since 1930). AT 3, Level 1–3

Fact or fantasy? Use the diary as a secondary source to identify what is known fact and what has been created by the author. AT 2, Level 3.

Discuss different points of view within the diary – for example, the Spanish viewpoint. AT2, Level 2-5

Using Will's diary for history teaching

Sequence events in the story and discuss story from historical perspective. AT 1, Level 1a, 2b,2c

Identify particular aspects of the diary which provide information and background to life in Tudor times – for example, life on board ship, Armada, transport, town life, children. AT 3, Level 1–5

Opportunity to examine key elements of photographs and pictures as primary and secondary source material. The diary contains photographs of original primary source material – for example woodcuts, tapestry, maps and artefacts – as well as secondary sources, such as Victorian paintings. Visual sources can be used to find out about the past and as a basis for discussion on how useful such resources are as evidence. AT 2, Level 4; AT 3, Level 1–5

However, his name has been borrowed from history and a fictional story weaved around it. It provides a context for the history.

There have been lengthy debates about the use of historical fiction in the teaching of history. But it is hard to deny that children, and adults, often become interested in history through fictional stories set in the past. Will's diary has been made as historically correct as possible.

The illustrations and photographs of artefacts, written sources, buildings and sites are intended to be used as primary and secondary source material.

For this reason the diary can be used directly for history teaching. It can also stimulate work in English. The two charts shown here examine some ways in which the diary can be used for English and history National Curriculum work.

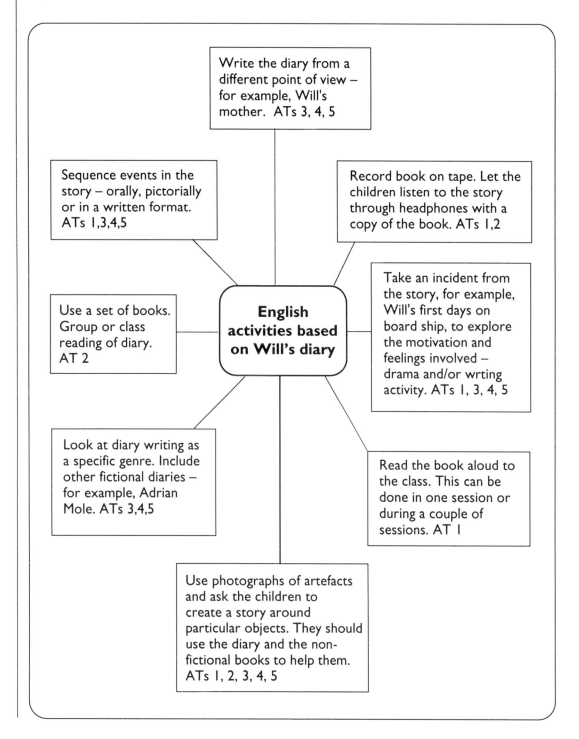

Write the diary from a different point of view – for example, Will's mother. ATs 3, 4, 5

Sequence events in the story – orally, pictorially or in a written format. ATs 1,3,4,5

Record book on tape. Let the children listen to the story through headphones with a copy of the book. ATs 1,2

Use a set of books. Group or class reading of diary. AT 2

English activities based on Will's diary

Take an incident from the story, for example, Will's first days on board ship, to explore the motivation and feelings involved – drama and/or wrting activity. ATs 1, 3, 4, 5

Look at diary writing as a specific genre. Include other fictional diaries – for example, Adrian Mole. ATs 3,4,5

Read the book aloud to the class. This can be done in one session or during a couple of sessions. AT 1

Use photographs of artefacts and ask the children to create a story around particular objects. They should use the diary and the non-fictional books to help them. ATs 1, 2, 3, 4, 5

Using the visual resource pack

Bringing history alive

The visual resources pack included with this Study Kit contains eleven colour posters which will be a key element in helping to bring history alive for the children in your class.

The posters will make ideal display material but they are also intended to be used as colourful primary source material for helping children to use evidence to find out more about the past.

If possible, the eight smaller, A4 sized pictures should be laminated so that they can be handled by the children for use individually or in groups.

Each of these smaller posters also has a description on the back which can be read to the children or which they can read for themselves. If you are using these posters for display, why not enlarge the descriptions on a photocopier and place them next to the pictures?

The Tudor family tree

The portraits used on the large A2 poster all come from the National Portrait Gallery and are all available from the gallery in postcard format.

Most primary schoolchildren will need teacher support when 'reading' a family tree like this one.

A key is provided for the symbols used but the whole design of family trees will also need to be discussed.

Older juniors and more able Year 3 and 4 children can discuss the Stuart line of the family tree, while teachers of younger juniors may feel that this amount of detail is not necessary so could make only brief reference to it.

The following activities will help the children to become familiar with using family trees:

- Ask the children to copy the pictures of the Tudor monarchs shown on the family tree on to separate sheets of paper. Can they put them in the right place on a horizontal or vertical timeline?

- Can the children make a simple family tree for the present royal family?

The Route of the Spanish Armada, 1588

This chart was published shortly after the Armada was defeated and, as well as showing the route that the fleet took around Scotland and Ireland, it also shows the wrecks on the Irish coast.

This provides a good visual source for looking at how map-makers of the time saw their country.

Only coastal towns are shown. Can the children explain why?

If possible, let the children look at county maps of their area during Tudor times so that they can compare the different mapping styles.

Comparisons can also be made between map-making now and then and the children could use an atlas to explore the differences in the ways in which map-makers saw the shape of different countries.

The children can also examine the symbols used on the map. If they look closely they can see that the map-maker has marked on the important encounters between the English and the Spanish fleets. This makes the map an active presentation of the retreat of the Armada, showing what happened over a period of time.

A similar technique is used in the painting of the Field of the Cloth of Gold (see below).

16th century Tudor farmhouse

This photograph was taken at the Weald and Downland Open Air Museum in Sussex and shows a reasonably-sized Tudor farmhouse.

The children may need help when examining and discussing the different elements of the photograph, such as the wooden windows with no glazing, the tiles, the chimney and the door.

For example, have they noticed the position of the chimney? It is in the middle of the roof and was probably added at a later date because we know that many Tudor houses simply had a hole in the roof to let smoke from a fire escape.

What about the tiles? Do the children think that these were put on the building when it was first built or were they added later?

It is more likely that the roof was originally thatch.

Next, the children could use reference books to find out more about the sort of furniture and tableware that would have been found inside the farmhouse.

Ask them to look closely at the inset illustration of the interior. How does this differ from the photograph as a form of evidence about the past?

The artist has included a range of pieces of furniture in the illustration to give the children as much information as possible about furniture design and style.

Would the farmhouse really have had so much furniture? What about the table-cloth?

Is there anything else that could be the artist's interpretation rather than fact?

The children can apply these same questioning skills to the pictures in the other text and reference books that they use.

Painting of the Field of the Cloth of Gold

It is thought that this picture was painted about 25 years after King Francis I and King Henry VIII met and that it records the event in accordance with evidence in contemporary written documents.

The colours of the picture are very dark and children will have to look closely to see that it contains a great many small details. Some children will find this challenging while others will need more help.

Ask them to:

● spot Henry

Ask the children to find out how many times they can see Henry VIII in the picture. He is most clearly seen in the procession at the bottom left of the picture but he can also be seen meeting King Francis at the top of the picture in front of the golden pavilion. In the upper right of the picture he can be seen again watching jousting with his wife Catherine of Aragon.

● find the dragon

There is a dragon in the top left of the picture which is thought to represent an elaborate firework or rocket which may

have featured in one of the many displays that took place.

● say what is permanent and what is temporary

The painting records, not particularly accurately, the towns of Guisnes and Hammes. Guisnes, shown on the left, was the English base. Hammes, with its castle, is on the right and this is where the French stayed. The picture shows clearly several tents. These provided meeting places, dining chambers for masques and banquets and sleeping quarters for kings, wives and servants.

● look for other evidence

Some children may be able to list the other sorts of evidence that this painting provides about life in Tudor times, such as clothing, entertainment, class differences and the virtual absence of women.

● think about now and then

Clearly, this painting is depicting a big political event and contemporary comparisons can be made with summit conferences. It was also a fantastic public relations event and the children will enjoy exploring the idea that this event was the Tudor version of a royal or pop star wedding today.

Laundresses at work

Along with the photograph of artefacts salvaged from the *Mary Rose* wreck (see below), this picture provides us with evidence of what domestic life was like in Tudor times.

It is incredibly difficult to find written or visual evidence about daily life and even this picture of laundresses is a German, rather than a British, representation of women at work. However, life in Britain at the time was probably very similar and the picture, which comes from the Harleian manuscript, does provide some good opportunities for children to discuss what is taking place and then suggest a sequence of events.

Interestingly enough, despite the title that the scene is given today – Laundresses at work – it is by no means certain that it really shows women washing.

Several historians have suggested that the picture might be showing cloth or linen manufacture.

There are several clues:

● First of all, the garments shown are uniform in cloth, width and length;
● The equipment being used is very elaborate;

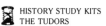

• The man on the left is throwing something onto the garments. This could easily be urine, which was used in Tudor times to bleach garments.

Are the children convinced by these arguments?

If the picture is interpreted in this way, it provides an opportunity to look at the work of women in the manufacturing process.

If the picture is interpreted as washday it can be used to discuss why washing clothes in this way would have been hard work. Some people still do their washing like this in many parts of the world.

Artefacts from the Mary Rose

The children can begin by identifying the different sorts of tableware shown in this picture of objects rescued from the wreck of Henry VIII's flagship, *Mary Rose*.

Can they suggest reasons why these particular objects have survived?

They could then compare the artefacts with the tableware seen in the picture of the Cobham family (see above right) and use reference books to find other domestic objects from the period.

The selection of pewterware includes few cutlery items. The idea that cutlery was rarely used in Tudor times is also supported by the Cobham portrait. We know that forks were virtually non-existent and that spoons were used only rarely.

Ask the children to find other references to the *Mary Rose*. Can they speculate why its discovery was so important in terms of the evidence it provided for life in Tudor Times?

Buckland Abbey

Along with the map of the River Thames (see opposite), this modern-day photograph can be used with the picture of the Tudor farmhouse to provide contrasting examples of Tudor housing.

Buckland Abbey, which was the home of Sir Francis Drake, is a good example of what happened to buildings as a result of the dissolution of the monasteries in Henry VIII's reign.

Wealthy families were able to buy up old abbeys and such buildings clearly

show the change of use from abbey to domestic house.

Can the children spot any evidence – like the benches – to show that the photograph was taken relatively recently?

Discuss how many historic buildings are now used as museums, and why.

Map of the River Thames

This London scene has plenty of detail. Ask the children to make a list of all the things that they can see.

The scene was painted several years after the Tudor period, and is dated 1650, but it illustrates what London was like at the time.

The human heads on the gate are one gory image which will appeal to the children but there are also several other small bits of information which can be drawn out from the picture.

For example, London Bridge is labelled 'The Bridge' simply because it was the only bridge at the time.

Road transport in the city was slow and it is possible to see several small ferry and cargo boats.

The large ocean-going boats can be seen on the right hand side of the bridge and this

was the only way in and out of the port of London.

The children might comment on the density of housing and the fact that several of the houses were several stories high. They are also likely to be surprised at the number of churches which can be seen and this can be linked to the importance of religion in people's lives in Tudor times.

The Cobham family portrait

Three portraits feature among the eight small posters in the visual resources pack and two of these have been chosen because they have children in them.

As *'Will's first battle'* shows, childhood in Tudor times did not really exist and children had to grow up very quickly, being sent out to work at a very young age.

It is often said that this is reflected in the representations of children in portraits.

However, although the Cobham children are dressed as adults, this is not really very different from today. How often do the children in your class wear similar clothes to their parents, such as track suits or jeans and T-shirts?

The closeness in the ages of the Cobham children is a reminder of the fact that, in Tudor times, most married women of child bearing age would have been pregnant almost constantly.

On the table we can see fresh fruit, such as pears, walnuts, cherries, grapes and apples.

This gives us a message about the Cobham family and overseas travel.

The exotic animals which two of the children hold are further clues.

Sir Walter Raleigh and son

This portrait of Sir Walter Raleigh and his son is an excellent starting point for looking at the messages that can be conveyed through a portrait.

For example, we can look at the stance of the people shown in the portrait, the facial expression, clothing, backdrop and furnishings.

Ask the children to try standing in the same pose as shown in the portrait.

What do they think that we are meant to conclude about the way these two people are standing?

Can they imagine what it would have been like to be the son of the famous Sir Walter Raleigh?

The portrait can be compared to other portraits of the period and similarities noted.

Not many Tudor portraits show a full-sized image, which probably tells us something about the tremendously high cost of commissioning a portrait and indicates the wealth of self-made men like Sir Walter Raleigh.

The Armada Portrait

It is believed that the Armada portrait of Elizabeth I was originally owned by Sir Francis Drake.

It shows the Queen richly jewelled and dressed.

Her right hand is resting on a globe. This is said to symbolise her new position as a figure of international power after the defeat of the Spanish Armada.

The crown, the symbol of monarchy, can be seen over Queen Elizabeth's right shoulder.

The picture is neither signed nor dated but the style of costume indicates that it was painted about 1580.

However, the ships in the windows behind the Queen are of a later period and this suggests that they were added in the following century.

The defeat of the Armada is shown in the left window while, on the right, the artist has painted a scene of the Spanish ships being wrecked on a rocky shore.

As with the illustrations of battles on the map showing the route of the Armada, the events in the two windows in this portrait show events that did not happen at the same time.

Like her father, Elizabeth was well aware of the importance of her visual image. As a result, there were several Armada paintings, all portraying her as a powerful and successful monarch.

However, it is believed that the Queen posed no more than eight times during her life which is why the face patterns are so similar.

Give the children the opportunity to compare different portraits of Queen Elizabeth I.

These portraits can also be used as a starting point for art work on portrait painting.

The children could go on to compare the Armada portrait with portraits from other periods in history. This will help them to identify clearly the Tudor style of portraiture.

The children could then paint their own portraits – either of themselves or of a friend or relative.

Can they suggest the type of symbols that their own portraits could show?

For example, T-shirts frequently indicate favourite teams, pop stars or cartoon characters.

Footnotes

English Heritage provides a wide range of guides on working in the historic environment.

[1] *History Through Drama* Viv Wilson and Jayne Woodhouse (The Historical Association). A teachers' guide which includes a description of a Tudor fayre, dramatised by children in Wiltshire at an authentic site in 1988.

[2] *Pot Luck* Jo Lawrie (A&C Black). Includes information on cooking and a selection of recipes from the past.

[3] **English Heritage** produces a series of seven books on food and cooking, one of which covers Tudor Britain. The books are available from English Heritage, PO Box 229, Northampton NN6 9RY.

[4] *A Teachers' Guide to Maths and the Historic Environment* Tim Copeland (English Heritage. How to carry out mathematical problem solving while visiting a historical site or building.

[5] *Historical Maps* Pat Hughes and Phil Tweedie (*Starting History* series, Scholastic Publications). Includes 56 photocopiable maps, teachers' notes and two full-colour posters.

[6] *A Teachers' Guide to Geography and the Historic Environment* Tim Copeland (English Heritage). Looks at the landscape at different historic locations, including ceremonial and religious sites, and provides case studies on selected places.

[7] *Circular number 6* (National Curriculum Council 1989). The National Curriculum and whole curriculum planning – preliminary guidance.

[8] *Women in Tudor and Stuart Times* (Islington Women's Equality Unit). A pack comprising activities and ideas that can be used as starting points and ways into a study of the period, with detailed sections depicting aspects of women's experience in Tudor and Stuart times. Contains resources and additional material. From The Women's Equality Unit, Town Hall, Upper Street, Islington, London N1 2UD (tel: 071 477 3134).

[9] *Farmers and Townsfolk* Peter and Mary Speed (*History Source Books* series, Oxford University Press). Provides Key Stage 2 pupils with details of many of the issues and events of the Tudor age. The following titles are also available in the same series: *The Queen, Nobles and Gentry*, *The Poor and the Wicked* and *Seamen*.

[10] *Elizabethan Dance* Peggy Dixon (*Dances from the Courts of Europe* series, Eglinton Productions). Two tapes of Elizabethan dance music with a booklet of instructions and background information on their social context in the period. From Eglinton Productions, 23 Carriagehill Avenue, Paisley, Scotland PA2 6LA. Also useful is *Tudor England* Alison and Michael Bagenal (*Music From the Past* series, Longman).

[11] *A Teachers' Guide to Using Portraits* Susan Morris (English Heritage). A comprehensive guide written for secondary teachers. Needs modifying for use with primary pupils.

[12] *Kings and Queens of England* (Fax-Pax). A set of 40 picture cards of kings and queens of England from the Norman Conquest to the present day. Each has a full-colour image of a monarch with details of important events on the reverse side. From Fax-Pax, PO Box 4, Perranwell Station, Truro, Cornwall TR3 7YX (tel: 0872 863544).

[13] *History in the Primary and Secondary Years* (HMI 1985 out of print). Offers a list of 95 concepts and ideas which HMI found were commonly used in history teaching with pupils up to 16 years of age.

[14] *Shakespeare stories* Leon Garfield (Gollancz). Re-written for primary children.

[15] *The Counties of Britain – A Tudor Atlas by John Speed* (Pavilion, out of print).

[16] Town maps from Tudor times may be available from local history libraries.

[17] *Town Mouse and Country Mouse* re-told by Molly Perham (*Favourite Tales series*, Ladybird). The tale of two mice who decide to try out each other's lifestyle.

[18] *Golden Hinde reconstruction*. For details of visits contact the *The Golden Hinde Educational Museum*, Salford Quays, Manchester M5 2SP (tel: 061 876 5974).

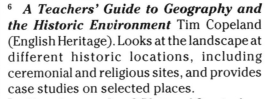

Other recommended resources

Packs and schemes

Tudor and Stuart Times, Topic Starter Pack (*Heineman Our World* series). Aimed at eight- to ten-year-olds, this is part of a comprehensive programme across Key Stages 1 and 2, involving topics such as religion.

Tudors and Stuarts Resource Pack Paul Noble (Collins Primary History). Includes some comprehensive teachers' notes and photocopiable worksheets for the children.

Tudor Life Red House Workshop (Anglia Young Books). This pack contains A4 black and white resource sheets, plus Teachers' Notes, and is intended to support *Under the Rose* – see **Children's Fiction**.

Junior Education August 1993 featured a 20-page Focus Pack on **Tudors and Stuarts**, plus a full-colour poster. Contact the Subscriptions Department, **Scholastic Publications Ltd**, Westfield Road, Southam, Leamington Spa, Warwickshire CV33 0JH (tel: 0926 813910).

A Sense of History – Tudor and Stuart Times Evaluation Pack Sallie Purkis and James Mason (Longman). Includes posters, timelines and audio cassettes, along with informaton on the political personalities and domestic life of the time.

Tudor and Stuart times (Ginn History). Intended for Key Stage 2, this pack includes a teachers' resource book with photocopiable sheets, a group discussion book and four colour pupils' books.

Using the Historic Environment (English Heritage Education Service). This is a free booklet that takes teachers through the process of discovering our historic environment, involving ideas and activities for local studies as well as detailing how conservation areas and listed buildings are established. From **English Heritage Education Service**, Keysign House, 429 Oxford Street, London W1R 2HD.

Books for children

Fiction

The Children of Green Knowe Lucy Boston (Puffin). The tale of a magic house inhabited by children from the past.

Under the Rose Alan Childs (Anglia Young Books). A Tudor spy story in which Crispin, a young baker's apprentice, is given a

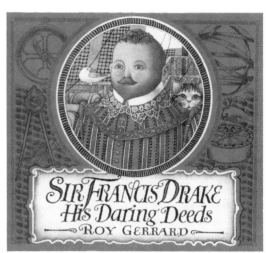

Cover of 'Sir Francis Drake His Daring Deeds' *(Gollancz).*

parchment by a dying beggar, and soon finds himself at the centre of a fiendish plot.

Sir Francis Drake His Daring Deeds Roy Gerrard (Gollancz). A children's picture book with rhyming text.

Non-fiction

Tudor Britain Tony Triggs (Wayland). Features some good quality colour photographs.

Tudor Sailors and ***Tudor Towns*** (*Begining History* series, Wayland). Photographs and artwork combine with the text to produce an insight into the lives of people of the time.

Sir Francis Drake, ***Henry VIII*** and ***Queen Elizabeth I*** (*Great lives* series, Wayland). Provides biographical information of these figures from the Tudor era, along with contemporary photographs and engravings.

Tudors Donna Bailey (*History Insights* series, Hodder and Stoughton). Covers many aspects of Tudor life, including education, entertainment, town life, trade, health and hygiene, houses and homes, religion and clothing. Features a wide range of colour photographs and illustrations.

Books for teachers

History 5-11 Joan Blyth (Hodder Headline). Discusses the content of each history study unit and suggests possible teaching approaches, including the use of historical drama.

Henry VIII – Images of a Tudor King Christopher Lloyd (Phaidon). A collection of colour photographs that combine with with the text to explore the life of this Tudor monarch.

Postcard collections

National Portrait Gallery Shop, St Martin's Place, London WC2H 0HE, supplies the *Tudor Kings and Queens Postcard Pack* which contains twelve colour portraits of the Tudor monarchs. The pictures include Henry VIII and four of his wives, Mary I and Philip of Spain. The pack also includes a 16-page booklet giving background information.

Videos

ETC, Leah House, 10a Great Titchfield Street, London W1P 7AA (tel: 071 580 8181) supplies *How We Used To Live: The Tudors*, a drama set in a Catholic household during the reign of Elizabeth I, supported by documentary. Also available from **ETC** is *Timelines: Tudors and Stuarts* a series of ten videos that explores aspects of life in Tudor and Stuart times, ranging from kings to farmers, medicine to food, technology to entertainment.

BBC Educational Publishing supplies *Tudors and Stuarts,* five videos that use re-enactments, 'living history' lessons and BBC costume drama clips to bring this period of history to life. For further information contact **BBC Education Information**, White City, London W12 7TS (tel: 081 746 1111).

Shropshire County Council Education Department, County Hall, Shrewsbury supplies *A Feast of History: Core Study Unit 2 – Tudor and Stuart Times.* Shows a Year 5/6 class investigating the topic, and covers a visit to Boscobel House.

The Tudor Kings and Queens Postcard Pack from the National Portrait Gallery includes 12 colour portraits of the Tudor monarchs.

Posters

National Portrait Gallery (address, see left) supplies *The Early Tudors and the Elizabethans Poster Pack*. A pack containing four colour portraits measuring 297 x 210 mm – two of Elizabeth I, one of Sir Francis Drake and one of William Shakespeare – plus eight pages of notes for classroom discussion.

Pictorial Charts Educational Trust, 27 Kirchen Road, London W13 0UD supplies *Tudors and Stuarts timeline* and also *The Civil War*, *The Elizabethan Court* and *Elizabethan Seaman*.

Software

ETC (address above) supplies *The Tudors and Stuarts*, a package containing maps, worksheets and computer datafiles about the period. BBC, Nimbus and Archimedes. Also available is *Heavy the Head*, an exploration of kingship in Tudor times and *BC – Before Chips*, a look at food through the ages. Archimedes.

Longman Logotron, 124 Cambridge Science Park, Milton Park, Cambridge CB4 4ZS (tel: 0223 425558), in association with the BBC, supplies *Landmarks – Elizabeth I* Steven and Ann Grand, (Archimedes, BBC, Nimbus and IBM), in which Betsy, a hard working housemaid in an Elizabethan manor house, takes you on a guided tour around the state rooms, kitchen, stables and garden during a visit by Elizabeth I.

Cambridgeshire Software House, Computer Centre, 8 Bramley Road, St Ives, Cambridgeshire PE17 4WS (tel: 0480 467945) supplies *Anatomy of a Tudor Warship 1520–1988: The Mary Rose* Ian Whittington, (Archimedes, BBC), a graphics driven simulation package that involves children in discovering for themselves many of the items that were found on the *Mary Rose*.

Note: Details of all the resources mentioned on these pages were correct at time of going to press.

Places to visit

Museums and galleries

National Portrait Gallery, St. Martin's Place, London WC2H OHE (tel: 071 306 0055). Has a range of paintings, including portraits of all the Tudor monarchs.

National Maritime Museum, Romney Road, Greenwich, London SE10 9NF (tel: 081 858 4422). Part of the museum is a seventeenth-century house, and there are many general items on display that date from the Tudor era.

The Museum of London, London Wall, London EC2Y 5HN (tel: 071 600 3699). Features a variety of galleries and displays with themes ranging from court life and trade to industry and religion in Tudor times.

British Museum, Great Russell Street, London WC1B 3DG (tel: 071 636 1555). Has a range of Tudor artefacts.

The Tower of London, Tower Hill, London EC3N 4AB (tel: 071 709 0765). Displays armour from the Tudor period and also has a lecturing centre (tel: 071 702 0013) that offers studies on the era.

Victoria and Albert Museum, Cromwell Road, South Kensington, London SW7 2RL (tel: 071-938 8500). Has several items from the Tudor era and also produces a leaflet detailing which artefacts in the collection relate to the Tudor section of the History National Curriculum at Key Stage 2.

Mary Rose Ship Hall and Exhibition HM Naval Base, College Road, Portsmouth PO1 3LX (tel: 0705 750521).

Tudor House Museum, Bugle Street, Southampton (tel: 0703 332513).

The Shakespeare Birthplace Trust's Properties, The Shakespeare Centre, Henley Street, Stratford-upon-Avon, Warwickshire CV37 6QW (tel: 0789 204016). These historic properties include: Shakespeare's Birthplace, Anne Hathaway's Cottage and the Shakespeare Countryside Museum at Mary Arden's House.

The Shakespeare Globe Museum and Rose Theatre Exhibition, Beer Gardens, London SE1 9EB (tel: 071 928 6342).

Ulster Museum, Botanic Gardens, Stranmillis Road, Belfast BT9 5AB (tel: 0232 381251). This museum has a large collection of artefacts from the wrecked Spanish ships *Girona* and *Trinidad Valencera* which were part of the Armada that threatened England during Elizabeth I's reign.

Historic houses and castles

Adlington Hall, Macclesfield, Cheshire SK10 4LF (tel: 0625 829206). Home of the Leghs of Adlington since 1315, the building is a quadrangular Manor House, featuring a great hall built between 1480 and 1505.

Arreton Manor, Arreton, Isle of Wight PO30 3AA (tel: 0983 528134). The manor was built between 1595 and 1612 and featuring examples of Tudor furniture.

Arundel Castle Arundel, West Sussex BN18 9AB (tel: 0903 883136/ 882173). Home of the Howard family which included Lord Howard of Effingham, who led the English fleet out to meet the Spanish Armada, and the third Duke of Norfolk, who was uncle to both Anne Boleyn and Catherine Howard. Features a collection of furniture and paintings, as well as personal possessions of Mary Queen of Scots.

Barrington Court , nr Ilminster, Somerset TA19 ONQ (tel: 0985 847777). Built between 1552 and 1564 by William Clifton, a prosperous London merchant, this house was restored in the 1920s by the Lyle family and is an example of the early-Elizabethan E-plan style of architecture.

Berkeley Castle, Gloustershire GL13 9BQ (tel: 0453 810332). Begun in 1117, the castle remains in the possession of the Berkeley family and features Elizabeth I's bowling green and terraced Elizabethan Gardens.

Bramhall Hall, Bramhall Park, Bramhall, Stockport, Cheshire SK7 3NX (tel: 061 485 3708). A Tudor house featuring furniture and wall-paintings from the period.

Broughton Castle, Banbury, Oxfordshire OX15 5EB (tel: 0295 812027). Originally built by Sir John de Broughton in 1300, the building was greatly enlarged between 1550 and 1600, when plaster ceilings, paneling and fireplaces were added.

Buckland Abbey, Yelverton, PL20 6EY (tel: 0822 853607). Formerly a thirteenth-century monastery, and then the home of Sir Francis Drake, the abbey includes monastic farm buildings and craft workshops.

Burghley House, Stamford, Lincolnshire PE9 3JY (tel: 0780 52451). Built in the sixteenth century by Sir William Cecil, later Lord Burghley, advisor and Lord Treasurer to Elizabeth I, the house has had few alterations and retains much of its original design and contains a large collection of art treasures.

Kenilworth Castle

Cotehele, St Dominick, nr Saltash, Cornwall PL12 6TA (tel: 0579 51222). A medieval house, remodelled by Richard Edgcumbe, who fought with Henry Tudor at the Battle of Bosworth. Features a late-Tudor great hall, with heraldic glass and a richly-moulded open roof.

Hampton Court Palace, Hampton Court, East Molesey, Surrey KT8 9AU (tel: 081 871 9750). Begun in 1514 by Cardinal Wolsey, with additions by Henry VIII and later by Christopher Wren and William III and Mary II. Tudor features include a state room, tapestries and pictures.

Hardwick Hall, Doe Lea, Chesterfield S44 5QJ (tel: 0246 850430). Late sixteenth-century house built for Bess of Hardwick, housing contemporary tapestries and furniture, and featuring walled courtyards.

Hever Castle, Hever, Edenbridge, Kent TN8 7NG (tel: 0732 865224). Childhood home of Anne Boleyn, and later in the possession of Henry VIII's fourth wife, Anne of Cleves, the castle features the Tudor-style Anne Boleyn's Garden as well as an exhibition in the Tudor Long Gallery of her life and times. Also includes a re-created Tudor village.

Kenilworth Castle, Kenilworth, Warwickshire CV8 1NE (tel: 0926 52078). Once owned by Robert Dudley, Earl of Leicester, a favourite of Elizabeth I, who in 1570 built a barn, gatehouse and palacial suite specifically for the Queen's visits. Elizabeth I's most famous visit in 1575 for nineteen days of festivities is celebrated in Sir Walter Scott's book *Kenilworth*. The castle was ruined in the civil war, although the barn remains intact.

Knole, Sevenoaks, Kent TN15 ORP (tel: 0732 450608). Dating from 1456 and enlarged by Thomas Sackville in 1603, the house features a collection of portraits and tapestries, and also a deer park.

Little Moreton Hall, Congleton, Cheshire CW12 4SD (tel: 0260 272018). A timber-framed moated manor house whose features include a long wainscoted gallery, chapel, great hall and knot garden.

Longleat House, Warminster, Wiltshire BA12 7NW (tel: 0985 844400). Built by Sir John Thynne with the help of mason-architect Robert Smythson, the house was completed in 1580, and still features its original great hall, as well as paintings and furniture.

Montacute House, Montacute, Somerset TA15 6XP (tel: 0935 823289). Late sixteenth-century house with an H-shaped ground plan with Rennaissance features that include contemporary plasterwork, chimney pieces and heraldic glass.

Penshurst Place, Penshurst, Nr Tonbridge, Kent TN11 8DG (tel: 0892 870307). With a history dating back over six centuries, the house features fifteenth-, sixteenth- and seventeenth-century paintings, tapestries and furniture, as well as the helm carried to St Paul's Cathedral in the state funeral procession of the Elizabethan courtier and poet, Sir Philip Sidney.

Speke Hall, The Walk, Liverpool L24 1XD (tel: 051427 7231). A half-timbered house, with a great hall and priestholes.

Temple Newsam House, Leeds LS15 0AE (tel: 0532 647321). Built around 1520 for Thomas Lord Darcy, the house has been altered by subsequent generations. It contains a panelled 'Tudor room' from Bretton Hall and other items of Tudor furniture.

Wollaton Hall, Wollaton Park, Nottinghamshire NG8 2AE (tel: 0602 281130). Now a natural history museum, this house was completed in 1588 by Francis Willoughby, a coal merchant, and was the work of the Elizabethan architect John Smythson.

Giant's Causeway, Bushmills, Co. Antrim BT57 8SU (tel: 026 57 31582). This coastal area features unusual basalt and volcanic rock formations, and was the wreck site of the Armada treasure ship *Girona* at Port-na-Spaniagh in 1588.

Giant's Causeway

Picture credits

Visual resource pack

Posters
Illustrations – *Sharon Pallent, Maggie Mundy Agency.*
Tudor monarch family tree:
National Portrait Gallery – Henry VII; Edward VI; Mary I; Elizabeth I. *Bridgeman Art Library* – Henry VIII.
Tudor farmhouse:
Weald and Downland Open Air Museum.
Chart showing the route of the Armada:
National Maritime Museum.

A4 Picture cards
Walter Raleigh and son: *National Portrait Gallery.*
Rural scene showing women washing: Harleian Manuscript, *by permission of the British Library.*
Armada portrait of Elizabeth I: *National Maritime Museum,* with permission of Sir William Tyrwhitt-Drake.
Pewter artefacts: *Mary Rose Trust.*
Buckland Abbey: *National Trust Photographic Library.*
Field of the Cloth of Gold: *Royal Collection Enterprises HM The Queen.*
Map of London showing London Bridge by Visscher: *Michael Holford.*
Portrait of Cobham family: *et Archive.*

Teachers' notes
Page 3 *National Trust*; Page 5 *John Harris*; Page 9 *Weald and Downland Open Air Museum*; Page 10 *Mary Evans Picture Library*; Page 11 *National Trust Photographic Library*; Page 13 *National Portrait Gallery*; Page 15 *Mary Rose Trust*; Page 17 (top) *Mary Evans Picture Library*; Page 17 (bottom) *National Trust Photographic Library*; Page 18 *English Heritage*; Page 20 *John Harris*; Page 34 *Gary Monkhouse*; Page 34 *National Trust Photographic Library.*

Background notes
Illustrations by Jane Bottomley.

The monarchy
Page 39 and 40 *National Portrait Gallery*; 41 (top) *Leicestershire County Council*, 41 (bottom) *Bridgeman Art Library*; 42 (top), *National Portrait Gallery*, 42 (bottom) *Scottish National Portrait Gallery.*

Court life
Page 53 and 54 (top) *Historic Royal Palaces, Hampton Court Palace*; 54 (bottom right) *Plymouth City Museum and Art Gallery*; 55 *National Portrait Gallery*; 56 *National Trust Photographic Library.*

Town life
Page 71, 72 and 73 (top) *Michael Holford*; 73 (bottom) *Micky Pledge*; 74 (top) *Leicestershire City Council*; 74 (bottom) *Mansell Collection.*

Rural life
Page 89 and 90 (top left and right) *Victoria and Albert Museum*; 90 (bottom) *Bridgeman Art Library*; 91 *et Archive*; 92 *National Portrait Gallery.*

Life at sea
Page 105 and 106 (top) *Michael Holford*; 106 (bottom) *The Golden Hinde Educational Museum*; 107 *National Portrait Gallery*; 108 (top left) *National Maritime Museum*; 108 (top right) *The Golden Hinde Educational Museum*; 108 (bottom) *Ministry of Defence.*

Religion
Page 119 and 120 (top) *National Portrait Gallery*; 120 (bottom) *Fotomas Index*; 121 and 122 (top) *National Portrait Gallery*; 122 (bottom) *Mansell Collection.*

Travel
Page 135 and 136 (top) *National Maritime Museum*; 136 (bottom) *British Library*; 137 (bottom) *Press Association*; 138 *Christies Images.*

Children
Page 149 and 150 *et Archive*; 151 *J Allan Cash.*

The Armada
Page 165 and 166 *National Maritime Museum*; 167 *National Portrait Gallery*; 168 *National Maritime Museum.*

How do we know?
Page 179 and 180 (top) *Mary Rose Trust*; 180 (bottom) *Plymouth City Museum and Art Gallery*; 181 *National Maritime Museum.*

Pupil record sheet

Name: _____

Lesson plan: _____

Date completed: _____

Concepts/Skills/Ideas	Comment
Observational skills	
Using historical language and ideas	
Asking historical questions	
Empathetic understanding	
Skills in chronology	
Using analysis of evidence	
Reference and information finding skills	

Figure 4

Homework sheet

Task:

Resources needed:

Approximate time to be taken:

Task completed satisfactorily
Signature of child:

Parent:

Teacher:

Any problems:

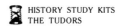

The Monarchy

Contents

The Monarchy

Background information

*F*or primary children, the most colourful monarchs of the Tudor era are King Henry VIII, with his six wives, and Queen Elizabeth I.

This may be the only knowledge with which some children are able to cope – while others may be able to provide a chronological record of key events in the Tudor period by the time they have finished this lesson plan. In between, the historical knowledge, skills, concepts and understanding that different children will achieve and be able to retain will vary widely.

However, studying portraits of monarchs is a good starting point for all children – irrespective of their ability – and also ensures that even non-readers will be able to gain some understanding of the concept of monarchy in Tudor times.

The House of Tudor

It was Henry VII who established the strong dynasty that was to rule England from 1485 to 1603. His success can be seen in the fact that he and his descendants all died peacefully in their beds rather than on the battlefield.

By the end of Henry VII's reign, the Tudor court was the sole centre of power in England. It is important to understand how this stability was achieved, for when Henry became king it was by no means certain that he would last any longer than those who had gone before him. Historians still argue about the main threats to his power. At one time it was thought that the most dangerous threats came from outside the royal household. Certainly, there were several rebellions and pretenders to the throne in the early years of Henry VII's reign.

Henry VII – the first Tudor king.

However, more recently, historians have looked more closely at threats from within the household. The truth is impossible to find. Even today, when the actions of famous people come under far closer public scrutiny, the lives of the royal family are still relatively secret.

How the Tudor monarchs gained power

Through the Royal Council

The mainspring of government was the Royal or Privy Council which contained more than 200 councillors who had taken a special oath to advise the monarch.

Clerics outnumbered nobles and Henry VII's most trusted adviser was John Morton, who eventually became Archbishop of Canterbury.

The Court of the Star Chamber was the centre of the Privy Council's judicial power.

Not all of these 200 councillors were full-time administrators although the great officers of State – the Chancellor, Treasurer and Privy Seal – were all full-time.

The Royal Council carried out a wide range of tasks and made no distinction between judicial and administrative business. Most surviving records show the council functioning as a court of justice. Cases were dealt with by a tribunal, sitting as the Court of the Star Chamber.

Heavy fines paid by wealthy landowners, who had fallen foul of the law, provided a useful source of revenue – as well as a means of blackmail. Occasionally, Parliament was summoned to raise further money as well as to crush those who challenged authority.

Through finance

Henry VII was extremely efficient in collecting money. He continued Edward IV's practice of by-passing the Exchequer, collecting his revenues and paying them directly to the Treasurer of his Chamber.

Crown lands, such as the Duchy of Lancaster, were exempt. They enjoyed a measure of independence and handled their own revenues.

Henry VII also established other ways of collecting revenue, which tended to hit at the land-owning classes rather than the growing merchant classes.

One of these methods was known as Morton's Fork – anyone who lived a flamboyant lifestyle was taxed because they were clearly wealthy while anyone who was known to spend their money carefully was taxed because they were believed to have savings.

By and large, Henry avoided having to ask Parliament for money, as parliamentary tax was liable to arouse great resentment and even open rebellion.

By the time Henry died, he was one of the richest kings in Europe and the Chamber was collecting nearly ten times as much as the Exchequer.

Through foreign policy

Wars cost money and the 100 Years War had drained the finances of the medieval monarchy.

However, the Tudor dynasty came to be more accepted by the European ruling families.

Increasingly, England was seen as an important market, a country gaining in power (also a source of expert seamen and navigators) and soon marriage negotiations with monarchies overseas were started.

A reconstruction of the Battle of Bosworth Field, at which Henry VII defeated Richard III.

Henry VII's eldest son, Arthur, married Catherine of Aragon, daughter of the King of Spain, while his own daughter, Margaret, married James IV, King of Scotland.

When Arthur died, Catherine of Aragon married Henry VII's second son, who became Henry VIII.

Key events

1485 – Henry Tudor defeated Richard III at the Battle of Bosworth and became King of England. His marriage to Elizabeth of York meant that the two opposing sides were now united and the Lancastrian and York houses were finally merged to form an alliance symbolised by the famous Tudor rose. The first years of Henry VII's reign were marked with conspiracies, rebellions and rival claims to the throne but, by the end of his reign, the Tudor dynasty seemed to be firmly established.

1509 – Henry VIII became king. He was Henry VII's third child and second son and so was not born to rule. However, his elder brother, Arthur, died in 1502 and shortly after his accession to the throne Henry VIII married Arthur's widow, Catherine of Aragon. They had several children but all except one died. She was called Mary. There are several reasons why Henry divorced Catherine in 1533 and then married Anne Boleyn. First of all, Catherine had not provided Henry with a son. However, the break from the Catholic Church, which was linked with his divorce, suggests other, more complex reasons. This is looked at in more detail in the section on the Break with Rome (see the section on *Religion*, starting on page 119).

By the time Henry VIII became king, the Tudor dynasty was firmly established.

1534 – Parliament declared Henry VIII Head of the Church of England. Cardinal Wolsey and Thomas Cromwell were key figures in this process. Sir Thomas More, who wrote the book *Utopia* in which he described the perfect state, was executed for failing to take an oath which declared that the King was the supreme authority in England rather than the Pope.

1536 – Anne Boleyn was executed, leaving behind one child – Elizabeth. The reasons for her execution were complex but it is unlikely that Henry would have divorced her had she been able to provide him with a son and heir. Henry's third wife, Jane Seymour, finally provided him with a son. She was the mother of the future Edward VI who was born in 1537. However, Jane never recovered from the birth and by the end of the year she was dead. Henry's next two wives – Anne of Cleves and Catherine Howard – continued the previous pattern: Henry divorced Anne of Cleves and executed Catherine Howard. During Henry's sixth and last marriage, to Catherine Parr, his health gradually deteriorated. The poison from an ulcer on his leg was spreading through his body and, in 1547, Henry died, leaving Catherine a widow.

1547 – Edward VI became king. He was only nine years old and depended heavily on the advisers who surrounded him. These men were Protestants and it was during Edward's reign that the first English Prayer Book was introduced. The dissolution of the monasteries, which had begun in 1536, had meant that schools attached to the monasteries closed. In Edward's reign, boys' grammar schools were started, ensuring that the sons of wealthy gentlemen were provided with an education. However, the majority of children still received no formal education. Despite his young age, Edward suffered from ill health and, in 1553, at the age of just 15, he

The execution of Mary Queen of Scots, 1587.

Queen Elizabeth I at the time of her coronation.

died, nominating Lady Jane Grey, his Protestant cousin, as his successor.

1553 – Mary, the rightful heir, became Queen. Mary is frequently presented as a weak and indecisive queen who was heavily dependent on the Catholic Church and her Catholic advisers. Certainly, she took a strong line against leading Protestant opponents and almost 300 people were burned at the stake because of their faith.

1558 – Elizabeth I was crowned. Elizabeth is probably the most interesting of all the Tudor monarchs. She was a strong and clever woman and during her reign there were several important political events which led to her prominence. The Elizabethan era is a particularly exciting one for primary children to investigate and Will's diary allows them to look at daily life during these times as well as one of the most spectacular events of the period – the Armada.

1587 – Mary Queen of Scots was executed. This event marked the ascendancy of Protestant power over Catholic power. Plots against Elizabeth continued but not on the same scale.

1588 – The Spanish Armada was defeated.

1600 – The latter years of the sixteenth century were marked by an expansion of trade. Then, in 1600, the Queen granted a charter to the East India Company enabling merchants to trade with India and the Spice Islands – the beginning the British Empire.

1603 – Elizabeth died and James VI of Scotland, son of Mary Queen of Scots, became James I of England, the first of the Stuart monarchs.

Lesson Plan : The Monarchy

Objectives

Classroom based activities
1. Provide an overview of the lesson to be covered.
2. Familiarisation with the concepts of monarchy, power and authority.
3. Knowledge of the chronology of the Tudor monarchs.
4. Skill in using portraits as primary source material.
5. Understanding of how such primary source material can be used as historical evidence.

Homework
1. Skill in using structural guides (contents, index, glossary) to select information about Tudor monarchs.

Resources

Reference books on Tudors, portraits of Tudor monarchs (provided), photocopiable research sheet for recording (provided).

Display

The activities in this lesson plan may be supplemented by the use and display of a published or teacher-created timeline showing pictures of Tudor monarchs and key events during their reigns. Reference can be made to the timeline throughout the lesson.

Lesson content

Introduction
General introduction to the whole unit involving:
1. asking children what they know about the Tudors and/or
2. providing background information about the Tudor monarchs in the form of the fact sheets on pages 44 and 45, or by asking the children to use reference books to find the answers to the questions on the research sheet on page 51.

Development
1. Drama work in which the children: take on the role of a monarch; create visible symbols of monarchy, such as a crown; discuss the power and authority of a monarch and the ways in which this is shown, for example subjects bowing before their monarch; explore factual and fictional monarchs; compare monarchy today with that in the

past. Activity sheet A provides an opportunity for children to record their understanding of the difference between fact and fiction.
2. Using portraits of Tudor monarchs to establish what they looked like and who they were and to create a simple Tudor family tree or timeline.

Extension activities
1. These could include looking in greater detail at one portrait. Activity sheet D suggests what to look for when studying a portrait.

Homework activities
1. Use reference books to create a timeline showing the major events in the life of one or more of the Tudor monarchs.

Assessment

AT I, Level 2c – Identify differences between monarchy today and in Tudor times.
AT I, Level 3c – Identify historical differences between Tudor monarchs.
AT I, Level 4c – Record different features of the Tudor period.
AT 2, Level I – Understand that Tudor kings and queens really existed while kings and queens such as Old King Cole and the Queen of Hearts are fictional.*
AT 3, Level I – Talk about what they see in a portrait of a Tudor monarch.*
AT 3, Level 2 – Recognise that portraits help to show us what Tudor monarchs looked like.*
AT 3, Level 5 – Comment on the usefulness of portraits as historical source material.
AT 3, Level 7 – Make judgements about the reliability and value of portraits as historical source material by reference to the circumstances in which they were produced.

* Suitable for lower ability levels

Fact sheet A

Name _____

Tudor kings

Henry VII (1457–1509)
Reigned 1485–1509

Henry VII became king in 1485 when he defeated Richard III at the Battle of Bosworth Field. This ended a civil war known as the **War of the Roses** and established the Tudor dynasty.

Henry VIII (1491–1547)
Reigned 1509–1547

Henry VIII had six wives.

When the Pope refused to allow him to divorce his first wife, Catherine of Aragon, the mother of Mary Tudor, Henry went ahead with his divorce anyway, making himself Head of a new Protestant religion known as the **Church of England**.

His next wife, Anne Boleyn, gave Henry a daughter – Elizabeth I. Jane Seymour, Henry's third wife, was mother of Edward VI.

Then followed Anne of Cleves, Catherine Howard and, finally, Catherine Parr – but Henry had no more children.

Edward VI (1537–1553)
Reigned 1547–1553

Edward was king for only a short time and died when he was just 15. Both he and his advisers were devoted Protestants. They made many changes to church services and introduced a new English Prayer Book.

Name _____

Tudor queens

Mary I (1516–1558)
Reigned 1553–1558

Mary married Philip II of Spain. She was keen to make England a Catholic country again and, during her reign, many people were killed for being Protestant.

Mary wanted children but was unable to have them and so, when she died in **1558** of cancer, her 25-year-old half-sister, Elizabeth, became queen.

Elizabeth I (1533–1603)
Reigned 1558–1603

Elizabeth was a strong and formidable queen. Unlike Mary I, she was a Protestant and became Supreme Governor of the Church of England. Elizabeth dealt very firmly with anyone who disagreed with her beliefs.

Elizabeth's religion and her relationships with other countries led to war with Spain, which included a great sea battle against the **Spanish Armada**.

Elizabeth died without having children, so the crown went to the Stuart family, under James VI of Scotland, son of Mary Queen of Scots.

Activity sheet A

Name _____

Fact or fiction?

Look at the kings and queens shown here.
Put a tick by those kings and queens who really
lived and put a cross by those who are made up.

Old King Cole

Queen of Hearts

King Arthur

Boudicca

Queen Elizabeth I

Queen Victoria

Name _____

Now and then

What is the same about these two pictures?

What is different about them?

Elizabeth I

Elizabeth II

Activity sheet C

Name _____

Tudor monarchs – timeline

Henry VII
1485–1509

Henry VIII
1509–1547

Edward VI
1547–1553

Mary I
1553–1558

Elizabeth I
1558–1603

_____

Use reference books to find out who had the crown:

● before Henry VII;

● after Elizabeth I.

Draw their pictures in the spaces provided.

_____

Name _____

Looking at portraits of Tudor monarchs

Choose a portrait of a Tudor king or queen.

Draw the portrait in this space and label it.

Why did you choose this portrait?

Describe the facial expression.

_____

Describe the clothes that the monarch is wearing.

Describe the monarch's pose or gesture. What does it tell you?

What other information does the portrait provide?

Make a list of things for a friend to find in this picture.

Activity sheet E

Name _____

The Tudor rose

Find a picture of the Tudor rose.
Draw the rose in the space below then colour it in.

Why were the white and red colours of the rose important?

Name _____

Tudor monarchs

Use reference books to find out about the Tudor kings and queens.

Write down the names of five Tudor monarchs and when they came to the throne:

_____ came to the throne in _____

_____ came to the throne in _____

_____ came to the throne in _____

_____ came to the throne in _____

_____ came to the throne in _____

Choose one of these monarchs and write down three events which happened during their reign.

Name of monarch _____

Event 1 _____

_____

_____

Event 2 _____

_____

_____

Event 3 _____

_____

_____

Assessment sheet

Name _____

I know the names of five Tudor monarchs:

1 _____

2 _____

3 _____

4 _____

5 _____

I know three major events that took place when these monarchs were on the throne:

1 _____

2 _____

3 _____

I have seen photographs of portraits of the following Tudor monarchs:

The portraits gave me information about:

	Tick	**Which portrait?**
What they ate		
What they wore		
What they were like to be with		
What jewellery they had		
What they liked to watch on television		
What games they played		
What happened in their reign		

Court life

Contents

Court life

Background information

*T*his section looks at Elizabethan court life and the way in which the nobles and gentry of the Elizabethan era lived. There are quite a few primary and secondary source materials available on this topic – although the picture they paint is not always one with which younger children can identify. Comparing royalty then and now is often the answer.

What was the Queen like?

There are several written sources describing Elizabeth I at various times during her reign. Some are extremely flattering and others fairly rude.

It is tempting to assume that the rude ones are more likely to be true.

However, children must learn to question any source of historical evidence by setting it in context.

Here are two fairly typical examples which were written towards the end of Elizabeth's reign.

'She wore a great red wig... Her face appears to be very aged. It is long and thin and her teeth are very yellow and unequal... Many of them are missing.'
French Ambassador, 1597

The children can compare modern-day pictures of Queen Elizabeth II with portraits of Queen Elizabeth I.

'Next came the Queen, in the sixty-fifth year of her age, very majestic, her face oval, but wrinkled, her eyes small, yet black and pleasant; her nose a little hooked, her lips narrow and her teeth black.'
German visitor, 1598

There are plenty of portraits of the Queen which can be used as primary source material. Of course, Elizabeth had final veto over the image presented by these portraits and the great similarity between them probably indicates that successful portrait painters had to flatter their subject.

Children can discuss whether they consider the pictures flattering today, and how fashions change with time.

Marriage and children

At the beginning of her reign, many of Elizabeth's political advisers assumed that she would marry and that her husband would take over the running of the country, so they set to work trying to find her a husband.

This is typical of the attitude towards women at the time. One of the main reasons why Henry VIII married six times was because he wanted to produce a son who could become king. Women were rarely seen as anything more than subject to their fathers or their husbands. Even Elizabeth often referred to herself as a *'mere woman'*.

It is tempting to see Elizabeth's refusal to marry from a modern feminist stance, as it certainly allowed her to continue as Queen in her own right. Many of her speeches also seem feminist. The much quoted speech that she made at Tilbury during the Spanish Armada is a prime example:

'I know I have the body of a weak and feeble woman, but I have the heart and stomach of a king, and of a King of England too, and think foul scorn that Parma or Spain or any Prince of Europe should dare to invade the borders of my realm.'

Elizabeth remained single and, by the time her child-bearing years were over, she was claiming that she was married to her country.

Sir William Cecil – one of Elizabeth I's most important advisers.

Elizabeth's advisers

Like her father, Elizabeth had several advisers who helped her to rule the country. Sir William Cecil, later made Lord Burghley, was one of the most important of these. It is difficult to gauge the influence on policy making of other favourites such as Charles Hatton, Robert Dudley or Philip Sidney, but Elizabeth was by no means the only monarch who had favourites and she seems to have been shrewd enough in her judgements to ensure that she lived to a good age, ruling a country which had considerably increased in its international standing.

Food at court

The domestic side of court life was run by three officers – the Master of the Horse, the Lord High Steward and the Lord Great Chamberlain.

Unfortunately, most of the palaces which Elizabeth used have been pulled down. Hampton Court Palace in London still exists but has been altered a great deal since the Tudor period.

However, the kitchens have been reconstructed to show them as they would have been in Henry VIII's reign, and written and visual evidence from these can be used to help children to appreciate the extent of the Tudor court.

Food was obviously a vital part of life but, among the wealthy, it was also important for entertainment.

The kitchens were central to palace life and would have been expected to feed hundreds of people. The Great Hall seated about 300 people and sometimes there would be two sittings. More important courtiers ate elsewhere and evidence shows that Henry VIII ate privately in his own rooms, fed from his own kitchen.

A visit to the kitchens at Hampton Court suggests that this was probably the only way to guarantee hot food because the kitchen was so far from the dining-chamber.

Wealthy Elizabethans ate huge quantities of meat and the average Tudor courtier consumed twice the number of calories taken in by the average person today. In one year, members of the Tudor court ate more than 1,240 oxen, 8,200 sheep, 2,330 deer, 760 calves, 1,870 pigs and 53 wild boar. Most of this would have been bought from local farmers and markets.

Less wealthy courtiers ate less meat. Many of their meals took the form of pottage, a thick broth made with meat and meat stock and thickened with herbs and cereals, such as oatmeal and barley.

Court life

There is plenty of written and pictorial evidence about the lives of the wealthy and the Elizabethan court.

We learn that Elizabeth loved plays, masques and pageants and that there was even a special official at court called the Master of Revels who was responsible for organising entertainment.

Dancing was another popular indoor entertainment and an additional Lesson plan is included in this section to help teachers to organise a Tudor dance session.

Several portraits show Tudor dance, and written sources, such as the one below, provide other contemporary evidence:

'She takes great pleasure in dancing and music. She told me that she kept at least 60 musicians. In her youth she danced very well, and composed measures and music, and had played them herself and danced them.'
Journal account from a French ambassador, 1597

Fox and hare hunting were popular sports and greyhounds were used for the chase. Bowls and cock fighting were also popular. Meanwhile, quieter leisure pursuits, such as needlework, reading and playing cards, were an important part of the gentlewoman's social timetable.

Several of Shakespeare's plays have been rewritten as stories for primary children[14]. One of these can be used in school as an example of the type of entertainment available in the court as well as in theatres such as the Globe in London.

Country houses

Many courtiers had their own country house or houses which often mimicked the court. They wanted their houses to look grand and many of those which have survived show that this was successfully achieved.

Many of the houses were built in the shape of the letter H or E to flatter King Henry VIII or Queen Elizabeth I. Others were built around a courtyard.

During Elizabeth's reign, the interiors of these houses became far more complex than ever before. More care was taken to ensure the privacy of the owner's family.

New bedchambers upstairs gave greater privacy at night time and it became more unusual for the family to eat in the Great Hall. As a result, records show that the Great Hall was often renamed the dining-chamber and was also used for games, dancing and plays.

Many large houses were built with walking galleries which could also be used for games, dancing, music and fencing.

Inventories show that the houses were sparsely furnished and the most prized pieces of furniture were beds.

Queen Elizabeth I had a water-closet installed in 1596 but it took some time before this idea caught on widely in the houses of the wealthy.

However, the gardens of these houses were designed with great care and increased overseas travel meant the addition of many new plants.

Buckland Abbey

Buckland Abbey – the family home of Sir Francis Drake.

This was Sir Francis Drake's home and still exists today. It is owned by the National

A typical Tudor garden.

Trust and is open to the public, so here children can see for themselves part of a house in which Drake lived and a number of his possessions.

As its name implies, the house was originally established as a monastery and was sold by Henry VIII when he took over the monasteries in 1539.

Some years after, Drake bought Buckland and it remained in his family for the next 370 years.

Most of the initial changes from abbey to country mansion were done by the previous owner. It is unlikely that Drake spent much time here.

A large colour photograph of Buckland Abbey is included in the visual resources pack with this Study Kit.

Furnishings

Few portraits give much idea of how Tudor houses were furnished. The real fashion for showing property did not appear until the seventeenth or eighteenth centuries.

We know that carpets were originally placed over tables but, by the end of the sixteenth century, they were used to cover the floor. The patterns and textures indicate their origins and the extent to which Tudor merchants travelled.

The portrait of Sir Henry Unton, which was commissioned by his widow – and is now in the National Portrait Gallery – is one of very few Tudor portraits which gives some indication of a person's domestic lifestyle. It shows a number of rooms in his home.

Lesson Plan : Court life

Objectives

Classroom based activities
1. Give the children enough knowledge of court life in Elizabethan times to be able to carry out further research independently.
2. Develop concepts related to the Tudor monarchy – in particular Elizabeth I.
3. Develop skills in using pictures and illustrations as primary and secondary source materials, concentrating on key elements of buildings and sites and portraits of the Queen, nobles and gentry.
4. Develop skills in using written source material to provide information about the past.

Homework
1. Ability to scan a newspaper for relevant information.
2. Compare and contrast past and present.

Resources

Photographs of Hampton Court, inside and out, and Tudor country houses (provided), plans of interiors of Tudor country houses, illustrations of palaces, such as Richmond and Nonesuch (provided), portraits and illustrations of Elizabeth I, her courtiers and court life (provided).

Display

Commercially-produced visual material, including that provided in this Study Kit, supplemented by children's pictures and writing, showing their ability to use historical source material.

Lesson content

Introduction
1. An examination of court life in Britain today. Children are asked to bring in newspaper cuttings which relate to the royal family. Production of a word bank relating to monarchy. Recording information.
2. Using photographs of portraits painted at the time and illustrations from reference books to provide examples of aspects of court life and the life of courtiers at home in their country houses.
3. Written sources as additional evidence (provided).
4. Recording information which

can be investigated further. This will depend on the source material available, for example costume, leisure activities, furniture, court festivities, Tudor buildings, food, daily life. Children can indicate areas where no information is available and discuss reasons why.

Development
1. Individually, or in groups, children can record one aspect of life in the Elizabethan court and give an individual or group presentation.

Extension activities
1. Children draw up a list of questions about one aspect of court life then tick those which can be answered from the source material.

Homework activities
Some newspapers, such as *The Times, The Daily Telegraph* and *The Independent,* have a section devoted to royal or court engagements. The children can use one of these and:
1. write down some of the activities which are similar to those that Elizabeth I would have done and some that she would not have done;
2. note anything that surprises them about the list.

Assessment

AT I, **Level 2c** – Identify differences between Elizabethan court life and today's Royal family.*
AT I, **Level 4a** – Recognise that some aspects of court life have stayed the same and others have changed.
AT I, **Level 4c** – Record different features of court life – for example, costume and food.
AT 2, **Level 4** – Show how the lack of evidence about Elizabethan court life might be one reason why pictures in different books show court life in different ways.
AT 3, **Level I** – Talk about what can be seen in a portrait of court life.*
AT 3, **Level 2** – Recognise that portraits can help to answer questions about court life in Elizabethan times.*
AT 3, **Level 3** – Make deductions about court life using the historical sources provided.
AT 3, **Level 4** – Put together information from primary and secondary source material to record a particular aspect of court life.
AT 3, **Level 5** – Comment on the usefulness of visual sources, such as court portraits, to provide a full picture of court life.
AT 3, **Level 6** – Compare the usefulness of the different source material provided when commenting on court life.

* Suitable for lower ability levels

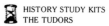

Fact sheet A

Name _____

Elizabethan court life

Nearly all the palaces that Elizabeth used have been pulled down so, to find out about court life in her reign, we have to gather evidence from several different sources:

- portraits painted at the time;
- illustrations and pictures drawn and painted later;
- descriptions written by people at the time;
- descriptions written by people later;
- reconstructions of aspects of court life – for example the kitchens at Hampton Court or television programmes.

The men and women who lived at court would also have had houses in other parts of England. Many built houses just in case Elizabeth came to visit them. Some of these houses still exist and give us more information about how wealthy people lived.

One of the most famous houses was built in Derbyshire by a woman known as **Bess of Hardwick**. Her official name was Elizabeth, Countess of Shrewsbury.

The house, which is shown below, is called **Hardwick Hall** and is owned by the National Trust so it is possible to visit it today.

Name _____

Royal palaces

Here is an illustration of one of Queen Elizabeth's palaces. It no longer exists. It was called **Nonesuch**, meaning *None like it.*

Elizabeth's main palace was **Whitehall** in Westminster. It stood by the River Thames in London and today there is a street known as Whitehall where the palace once stood.

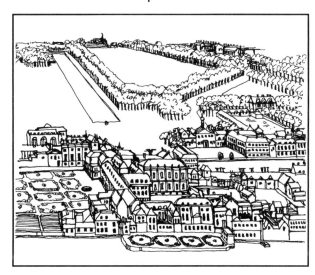

The most important part of any palace was the **Great Hall** where grand ceremonies were held. Here is an illustration of the Great Hall at **Hampton Court Palace**.

Activity sheet A

Great houses

Here is a plan of the Great Hall at **Rufford Old Hall** in Lancashire as it is today.

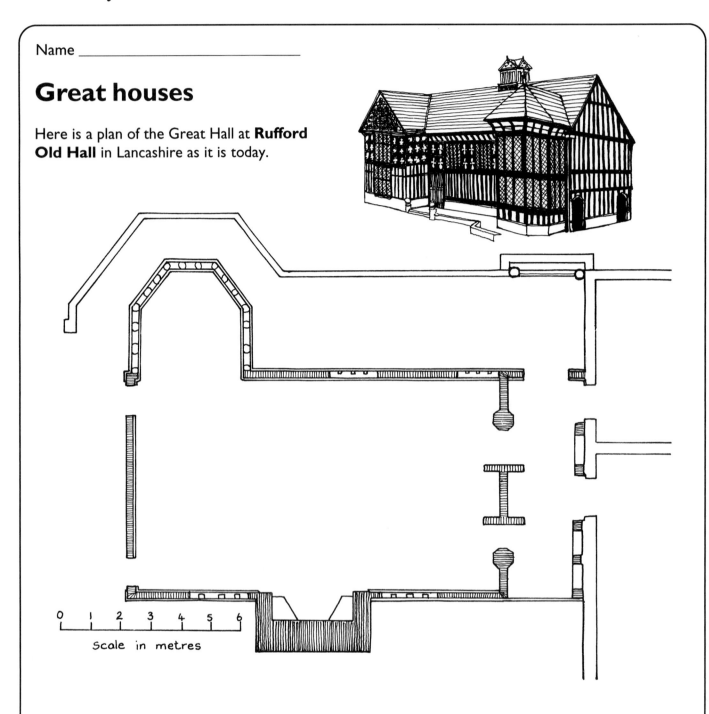

```
0   1   2   3   4   5   6
Scale  in  metres
```

We know that, in 1620, the Great Hall at Rufford contained these things:
30 pictures, 1 long table, 2 benches, 1 table in the compass window with a cloth, 1 drawing table with a carpet cloth and 2 forms, 16 cushions, 7 stools and 3 chairs, 1 green hanging on a curtain rod, 1 pair of tables, 1 screen, 1 pair of snuffers.

Use this information, and any pictures of Tudor furniture that you can find in reference books, to draw a picture of how the Great Hall might have looked.

Think of two different sorts of hall that you know today. Draw up two inventory lists for these halls.

Why were many Tudor houses built in the shape of a letter E or H?

Name _____

A royal procession

Here is a written source from 1598 which
describes a ceremony at Elizabeth's court.

'We were admitted into the Presence
Chamber, hung with rich tapestry, and
the floor, after the English fashion,
strewed with hay. It was Sunday when
there is usually a crowd of nobles....They
were waiting for the Queen to go to
chapel....She was attended in the
following manner –
First were gentlemen, barons, earls,
knights of the Garter, all richly dressed
and bareheaded; next came the
Queen....the ladies of the court following
her, for the most part dressed in white.
She was guarded on each side by
gentlemen pensioners, 50 in number,
with gilt battle axes.'
From Paul Hentzner's *Account of a Visit to England*

Underline any words in the passage
that you do not know and find out what
they mean. Put a circle around them if you
still cannot find out.

In the space below draw a plan of the royal
procession described. What other information
would you need to know if you wanted to
paint a picture of this scene?

Find a painting of a royal procession. Write
down three difficulties that the painter might
have had when painting this picture. Do you
think it is an accurate source of evidence?

Activity sheet C

Name _____

Costume

When Elizabeth died she left 3,000 dresses.
A short while before she died she made an
inventory of her clothes. These are just a few
items from the list:

Robes	99
French gowns	102
Round gowns	67
Loose gowns	100
Kirtles	126
Petticoats	125
Cloaks	96
Bodices	85
Fans	27

Note: A **kirtle** is a bodice and a skirt which is
open down the front.

Write down three things in this portrait which tell us that Elizabeth was a Tudor monarch:

1 _____

2 _____

3 _____

Find two different portraits of Elizabeth.
Draw or describe the dresses she is wearing in them.

Name _____

Ruffs

Ruffs started out as a small frill around the neck but when starch was introduced they were made larger and larger. The loops in the ruff were called sets.

Here is a description of a ruff that was written during Elizabeth's reign by a puritan called **Philip Stubbes**:

> 'They have great and monstrous ruffs made of the finest cloth that can be got for money. Some be a quarter of a yard deep, some more, very few less. The Devil in the fullness of his malice first invented these great ruffs.'

Why do you think that a puritan might describe ruffs as being the invention of the Devil?

Write down what you would consider to be two bad things about wearing a ruff:

1 _____

2 _____

Write down three modern forms of neck-wear which a Tudor person might find surprising:

1 _____

2 _____

3 _____

Activity sheet E

Court festivities

Written sources tell us that Elizabeth and her courtiers loved plays, masques and pageants. **William Shakespeare** belonged to a company of players called the Lord Chamberlain's Men and acted in plays in Elizabeth's presence. Several of his plays were written specially for her. *Midsummer Night's Dream* was written for a wedding she attended and *Twelfth Night* was played before her one Christmas.

What is a masque? Why do you think people enjoyed them?

Find out the names of some of William Shakespeare's other plays.

Use reference books and pictures to find out what other entertainment a courtier would have enjoyed. Write down as many of them as you can.

Name _____

Woman in a man's world

Many of Elizabeth's courtiers spent many years trying to find The Queen a husband, believing that it was not a woman's job to run the country. Look at this passage from one of Elizabeth's speeches.

What evidence do we have that Elizabeth was not 'weak and feeble'? Why do you think that she said she was 'weak and feeble'?

> *'I know I have the body of a weak and feeble woman, but I have the heart and stomach of a king, and of a King of England too, and think foul scorn that Parma or Spain or any Prince of Europe should dare to invade the borders of my realm.'*
>
> Queen Elizabeth at Tilbury, 1588

Lesson Plan : Tudor dance

Objectives

Classroom based activities
1. Knowledge about Tudor music and dance.
2. Develop skill in examining written and visual source material to find out about Tudor dance.
3. Appreciation of the skills involved in Tudor dance.
4. Empathetic understanding of one of the leisure pursuits of Tudor courtiers.

Resources

Elizabethan music[10].
This session is best carried out in a hall or gymnasium where there is plenty of room.

Display

Pictures of Elizabethan court dance (provided), descriptions by children of what it felt like to do the dancing, photographs or video of the children performing.

Lesson content

Introduction
1. Show the children pictures of Elizabethan dancing (provided).
2. Ask them what they think is going on in the picture.
3. Ask them to compare modern-day dancing with the dance shown in the picture.

Development
1. Listen to Elizabethan music.
2. Walk in procession to the music.
Remind the children of the sorts of clothes they would be wearing if they were Tudor courtiers, particularly ruffs, which would raise their heads.
3. Give the children time to get used to the music, concentrating on body stance. Reinforce the concept of monarchy by placing an empty chair on a raised dais and ask the children to walk forward and bow or curtsey to it. This is known as the **reverence** (see page 67). This provides an opportunity to develop concepts of power, hierarchy and allegiance.
   In the dance called the **pavane**, both partners do the same step. Details about the dance steps are provided on page 16.

Extension activities
1. Use written and visual sources to provide additional material about Tudor dance (see Fact sheet, page 67). Let the children describe the sort of skills they think this sort of dancing would promote.

Assessment

AT I, Level 3c – Identify the differences between the Tudor dance undertaken in class and the sort of dancing taking place today.*
AT I, Level 5c – Discuss how clothing and courtly procedure influenced Tudor dance.
AT 2, Level 2 – Using the written sources provided, show how different observers described Tudor dance.
AT 3, Level I – Talk about what can be seen in a picture of Tudor dance.*
AT 3, Level 2 – Recognise that written and visual sources can help answer questions about the past.
AT 3, Levels 3 and 4 – Use the variety of sources provided, as well as the experience of doing the dance, to make simple deductions about what Tudor dance was like.

* Suitable for lower ability levels

Name _____

Tudor dance

We know of four dances performed at the court of Elizabeth I, although there were probably others.

Our evidence comes mostly from eyewitness accounts and from art and music from the period.

We can only guess whether or not these dances were performed by people in the middle classes or in rural areas. Undoubtedly, peasants had their own forms of dance.

Dance was a prominent feature of any celebration and was seen as one way of displaying wealth and position in society. Elizabeth I was reputed to be a good dancer.

The four dances we know about are:

The pavane – a slow, stately dance often involving a procession;

The galliard – a dance for men – women joined in but only to admire the men performing;

The almaine – a lively circular dance for men and women;

The volta – a very athletic dance, only for the really energetic.

The reverence
This was a greeting or a way of thanking a partner in a dance.

With back straight, the man stepped back on his right leg which was bent and, keeping the front leg straight, he bowed stiffly at the waist.

The lady did what is called a *demi-plié,* with a bending of the knees, heels together and toes turned out.

A look at the costumes worn in this period is a good reminder of how movement would have been restricted.

Basic dance steps
These were known as **simples** and **doubles**.

Simple – This is just one step either forwards, backwards or to the side which is followed by closing the other foot to it, without placing any weight on the ground with the following foot. It counts for two beats.

Double – This is three steps and a close, again with no weight on the following foot. It counts for four beats and can be forwards, backwards or to the side.

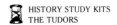

Activity sheet A

Name _____

The basic pavane

Here is a basic **pavane** sequence. It should be
done in column formation, facing the Queen
who is symbolised by an empty chair.

1 Simple to the left
2 Simple to the right
3 Double forwards, starting with the left foot
4 Simple to the right
5 Simple to the left
6 Double backwards, starting with the right
   foot.

Start from 1 again.

Gentlemen stood on the left, with the palm of
their right hand facing forwards. The lady
would place her left palm in his right palm.

The gentleman controlled all the movements
and the lady followed him.

Discuss how these positions reflect the status
of women in society.

One reason why the man stayed on the left
was because he would be wearing his sword on
his left side. He had to make sure that his
partner did not get caught up in the sword and,
if he needed to draw his sword, the lady would
not be in the way.

Name _____

Tudor dance

'I was stayed two days longer, til I might see her dance, as I was informed. Which being done, she (Elizabeth) enquired of me whether she or my queen (Mary Queen of Scots) danced best. I answered that the queen danced not so high or as disposedly as she did'.

Sir James Melville of Halhill, at court in 1564

Which dance do you think Sir James is talking about?

Who does he work for?

What information about Elizabeth does her question to Sir James give us?

Sir James' reply was very **diplomatic**. How?

Can you think of an occasion when you have had to give a diplomatic answer to a question?

Assessment sheet

Name _____

I have used these sources to find out about what life was like in the Court of Elizabeth I:

The most useful source of evidence was:

One of the difficulties of using these sources to find out information about the past is:

I have used these sources to find out what life is like in the court today:

One of the difficulties about finding out about court life today is:

Town life

Contents

Town life

Background information

Children learning about town and country life in Tudor times can begin by finding out exactly what is meant by the two concepts. Today, urban sprawl and the increasing number of housing estates attached to small villages have made the distinction between the two much less sharp. The terms *town* and *country* are also relative and so should be explored in relation to the children's experience. Many modern country villages would have seemed like huge towns in Tudor times, so the concepts of town and country will also need to be redefined in historical terms. Maps of Tudor towns can help.

The population of England and Wales at the time of Elizabeth I was around 3,250,000.

Some of the largest towns were on the coast and were important ports (**Figure 1**).

Figure 1

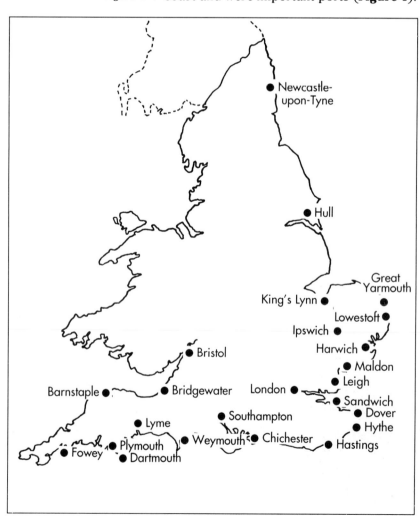

In the town

Tudor towns would have seemed very small to us and maps drawn at the time show that many of them had only a few hundred houses.

In the middle of most towns there was a church, and some towns would also have had a school for the sons of gentry. Most of the houses would have been small, thatched cottages with no chimney, so any smoke would have had to find its way out through a hole in the thatch.

One of the major problems faced when discussing town life in Elizabethan England is that each town was very different. Therefore, it is best to concentrate on researching the history of the nearest town to your school.

This is far more relevant and interesting to the children than a superficial overview of Tudor towns.

Investigating street names is one simple way of providing evidence of the past. But beware – Tudor Walk and Tudor Row could be streets in a new estate of detached, mock Tudor houses with no real historical background.

Local record offices and libraries often produce reconstructed town plans and area maps for the Tudor period or slightly later and these make excellent visual source material for children, particularly those who have difficulty with reading. It is also worth putting some pressure on local library and museum education services to encourage them to adapt their materials for primary children, if they have not already done so.

Focus on London

Many books describing town life in Tudor England write about London as if it was the only town in the country. This is probably because source material is more easily available for London and includes several maps of the city. These maps show how small London was compared to today and also show that there were still plenty of green, open areas.

But London life was no more typical of the rest of the country than it is now. It was

This map of London, drawn in 1650 by an artist called Visscher, shows houses and shops built across London Bridge.

certainly the largest English town and, by Elizabeth's reign, had at least ten times the population of any other English town and was bigger than any other town in northern Europe. It was also growing rapidly.

A survey of the city written in 1603 records some of the disadvantages of its rapid growth:

'this common field, being once the beauty of the City....has many filthy cottages and laystalls upon it. In some places the road is not wide enough for carriages and droves of cattle to pass'.

The same survey tells us that the Fleet river had become *'worse cloyed and choken than ever it was before'* because of the *'casting of soilage into the stream'*.

Within the city walls, houses were narrow and tall so that as many as possible could face on to the street. Fynes Moryson, writing in 1619, records:

A Tudor house in Plymouth.

'At London the houses are very narrow in the front towards the street, but are built five or six storeys high, usually of timber and clay with plaster, and are very roomly inside.'

At this time, some houses were even built on London Bridge and half way over there was a drawbridge which was pulled up to allow ships to pass through or to keep people out of the city.

A large colour picture of the contemporary illustration shown above is included in the visual resource pack in this Study Kit.

Life in Plymouth

Will's First Battle is set in Plymouth which was a busy and growing town in Elizabethan times. As can be seen from the map in **Figure 1**, it was one of the largest towns in England and Wales.

Its position as a port meant that ship merchants, sea captains and adventurers would all have been walking its streets and wanting somewhere to live. As a result, the population of Plymouth doubled between 1575 and 1600.

A Tudor house like the one mentioned in Will's diary has survived until today and can be seen in Plymouth. Now known as the Elizabethan House, it was built around 1584. Fact sheet B in this topic section provides an artist's impression of the interior of such a house.

However, fishermen and poorer people lived in smaller houses, perhaps nearer to the quay, while archaeological evidence shows that servants and apprentices were housed in little cottages, often built in back gardens.

The house opposite the Elizabethan House in Plymouth was built at the same time. Its overhanging windows were designed to catch as much light as possible because houses were built so close together. This also made the streets dark as well as dirty and smelly. Rubbish was thrown out from people's houses

Leicester Guild Hall – a fine example of Tudor architecture.

and, in many towns, open sewage flowed along the street.

Law and order

Law and order were strictly enforced by the mayor, leading members of trade guilds, shopkeepers and other important citizens.

Initially, *guilds* were formed by groups of traders who made rules about how their trade was carried out. They met in Guild Halls which have survived to the present day in some towns. Evidence of others survives in the names of streets and lanes.

Leading guild members formed an important part of the local power base. They were responsible for making laws and ensuring that these were enforced. There were laws for every area of town life:

Trade

There were laws regulating length of apprenticeship, markets, standards and prices and the exclusion of foreigners, including not only beggars and vagrants from elsewhere but, more importantly, competition from other crafts people.

Moral welfare

Towns were hard on undesirables and records show that there were frequent hangings in towns such as Plymouth. In 1578, a man named Clark was hanged and from written records we know that this cost 11s 2d (7s 6d for the gallows, 4d for carrying the ladder and 3s and 4d for the hangman). At the time, farm labourers were paid only about 1d or 2d for one day's work!

The ducking-pool in the harbour was also in frequent use and many undesirable people were dumped over the town boundary to be sent on to the next town. The records for Plymouth show some interesting gender differences here, with undesirable females being dumped in one particular area.

There were also laws about clothing and people who broke these laws were fined. In 1561, an Exeter apprentice boy was fined when he was found strutting about in ruffs and a silken hat.

Health

The order books of many towns had regulations *'to warn inhabitants to keep channels against their houses free from filth'* or against making *'dunghills out of stables in the street'*.

But generally, health had low priority and there is plenty of evidence to show that little was done to keep towns clean except when plague was raging or imminent.

Pure water was almost unknown outside country towns or villages which were fortunate enough to have a clean river or well.

Some towns would have had a doctor but his services would have been expensive and so the majority of the population depended on home remedies or the services of a local wise woman.

Of the doctors that did exist, few had any training and cures were often more fatal than the disease.

The ducking pool.

Lesson Plan : Town life

Objectives

Classroom based activities
1. Knowledge about aspects of Tudor town life, such as housing and street patterns.
2. Developing concepts related to bias, class, continuity, change, economy, law, evidence.
3. Skill in using primary and secondary source material to obtain evidence about life in Tudor England.
4. Ability to distinguish between the lifestyles of different classes.
5. Asking historical questions using historical language.

Homework
1. Using primary and secondary source material to answer historical questions.

Resources

Reference books about Tudor towns, local county map for example by John Speed, local town map, if available, for Tudor era, other locally-based written and visual source material for the Tudor period.

Display

Then and now display, showing aspects of Tudor town life, such as Plymouth in the Elizabethan era. Tudor town project booklets showing evidence of life in Tudor England.

Lesson content

Introduction
1. Using illustrations in Will's diary and reference books to find out about Tudor town life, concentrating on streets and house exteriors and interiors. The research sheet on page 87 provides a map of Plymouth.
2. Noting what can be seen in illustrations of street scenes and house interiors.
3. Identifying some of the difficulties involved in finding out how ordinary people lived – lack of source material; dangers of making generalisations; the dangers of simplifying complex and varied lifestyles.

Development
1. Examining photographs of local areas in the recent past. Recording the changes in housing and streets. Finding out what it looked like 400 years ago, perhaps using a map of the area near to the school that was drawn up in Elizabethan times.
2. Identifying any local evidence of a Tudor legacy, such as mock Tudor facades on new houses, as well as genuine remains of Tudor buildings.
3. Examining a modern street plan of local towns and comparing it with a street plan of a Tudor town.

Extension activities
1. Devising a time capsule box. Suggesting/collecting ten artefacts which would show someone in the future what life is like today. Recording this pictorially.
2. Examining and recording features or activities of a town today and noting those that would not have been present in Tudor times. The emphasis here is on continuity.

Homework activities
1. Using reference books to find out about Tudor town life.
2. Using the project sheet to devise a question about an aspect of Tudor town life, such as house interiors.

Assessment

> **AT I, Level 2c** – Identify differences between an Elizabethan town and the nearest town to the school.
> **AT I, Level 3a** – Describe how towns have changed since the Elizabethan era.
> **AT I, Level 3b** – Suggest a reason why.
> **AT I, Level 4a** – Recognise that some things in Elizabethan towns were the same as they are today.
> **AT I, Level 4c** – Arrange, label and display pictures, maps and diagrams which illustrate aspects of town life in Tudor Britain.
> **AT 2, Level I** – Understand that real people lived in the Tudor era.*
> **AT 2, Level 2** – Understand that we might think differently from people who wrote at the time.
> **AT 2, Level 4** – Show how the lack of evidence about the lives of ordinary people results in texts and pictures in different books showing life in different ways.
> **AT 3, Level I** – Talk about or record what they can see in a picture of a Tudor town.*
> **AT 3, Level 2** – Show how a written source, such as a map, can provide evidence about the size of an Elizabethan town.
> **AT 3, Level 3** – Make simple deductions about domestic life using sources provided.
> **AT 3, Level 4** – Use information from a number of historical sources to record one aspect of town life in Tudor times.
> **AT 3, Level 5** – Comment on the usefulness of a black and white line drawing showing a feature of Tudor life.
> **AT 3, Level 6** – Comment on the usefulness of a variety of written sources to describe life in Tudor Britain in the area around the school.
>
> * Suitable for lower ability levels

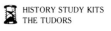

Fact sheet A

Name _____

Town life

Elizabethan towns were much smaller than
towns are today. Many were still surrounded
by walls and people went in and out of the
town through big iron gates which were closed
at dusk. The streets were very narrow and
houses were built so that the first floor jutted
out beyond the ground floor and the second
floor jutted out beyond the one below.

   The streets were also dark, dirty and
smelly. Rubbish was left in front of houses and
sewage often flowed in open drains.

THE BEAR

Name _____

Elizabethan house

These two illustrations show the outside and
the inside of an Elizabethan house in Plymouth.

Fact sheet C

Name _____

Using written sources: Furniture

William Harrison wrote a description of England in 1577. In the extract on the right he is describing the furniture that he has seen in towns.

Note: *Turkey work* refers to carpets from Turkey. At first these were used to cover tables but later they were used on the floor.

'Likewise in the houses of knights, gentlemen, merchantmen and some other wealthy citizens, it is not uncommon to behold generally their great provision of tapestry, Turkey work, pewter, brass, fine linen and costly cupboards of plate worth £500 or £600 or £1000....'

Name _____

Date _____

Question(s) to be answered:

Answer(s) - continue on back of sheet if necessary:

Books used:

Other source material used:

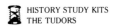

Research sheet

Name _____

Using evidence to find out about Tudor England

We can use different sorts of evidence to find
out about life in Tudor England:

Written evidence such as:

Buildings and sites such as:

Pictures and portraits such as:

Artefacts such as:

What other evidence did you use when finding out about life in Tudor times?

What kind of evidence was difficult to find?

Name _____

Using written sources: Local officials

Written sources can tell us something about town life in the Tudor period.

Many towns appointed officers to look after the town. In Prescot in Lancashire there were 15 officers. Two of these were known as **Streetlookers**. These men had to make sure that the people of the town disposed of their rubbish properly, including their sewage.

There are many written records of people being fined when they did not keep the town clean. Prescot court records show that, in 1558, a man called Richard Bower was fined 3s 4d.

> 'for making a midden unlawfully in the street, of unseemly aspect and unhealthy odour, to the great disturbance of neighbours and others'.

Activity sheet A

Name _____

Then and now

<table>
<tr>
<td>

Then
Here is an illustration of Will,
the character from the diary,
standing in the street.

</td>
<td>

Now
Here is a picture of a nine-year-old boy
standing in a street today.

</td>
</tr>
</table>

Note down:
Any differences

Any similarities

Name _____

Tudor markets

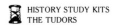

You can find colour illustrations of Tudor markets in **Will's first battle**.

Write down five things that you can see in the picture above which tell you that this is not a scene from a market today:

1 _____

2 _____

3 _____

4 _____

5 _____

Activity sheet C

Name _____

Elizabethan theatres

James Burbage built the first theatre just
outside London in 1576.

Later, when it was reconstructed, it was
renamed the **Globe**. Shakespeare's company of
actors performed many of its plays there. All
the female roles were played by men.

Now   **Then**

Write down three differences between the two theatres:

1 _____

2 _____

3 _____

Why do you think men played female roles?

Use a reference book to find out two more things about the Globe.

Name _____

Different life styles

Not everyone lived in exactly the same style in Elizabethan England. These illustrations show three different houses that would have been found in Elizabethan towns.

Which house do you think is most likely to have survived until today?

Write down four things which have made domestic life easier today than it was in Tudor times:

1 _____

_____

2 _____

_____

3 _____

_____

4 _____

_____

Write down four things which a Tudor child might find very strange in your house:

1 _____

_____

2 _____

_____

3 _____

_____

4 _____

_____

Activity sheet E

Name _____

Begging

'...if any other person or persons come to any man or woman's door to beg then the same man or woman to give unto the same beggar no manner alms or relief but rather bring or send him to the stocks within the same ward, or else to deliver him to the constable.... and he to put him in the stocks and there to remain by the space of a day and a night.'
From regulations made at Chester in 1539

What information does the picture of the whipping post give us?

What additional information does the written source give us?

Are beggars punished like this today?

What is the main difference between punishment today and in Tudor times?

Use a reference book to find out more about the work of a constable in Tudor times.

Name _____

Plymouth in 1539

Here is a map of Plymouth made in 1539. It was made by putting together a lot of little maps.

Write down the names of the places which are marked.

What other information does the map give you about Plymouth in the sixteenth century?

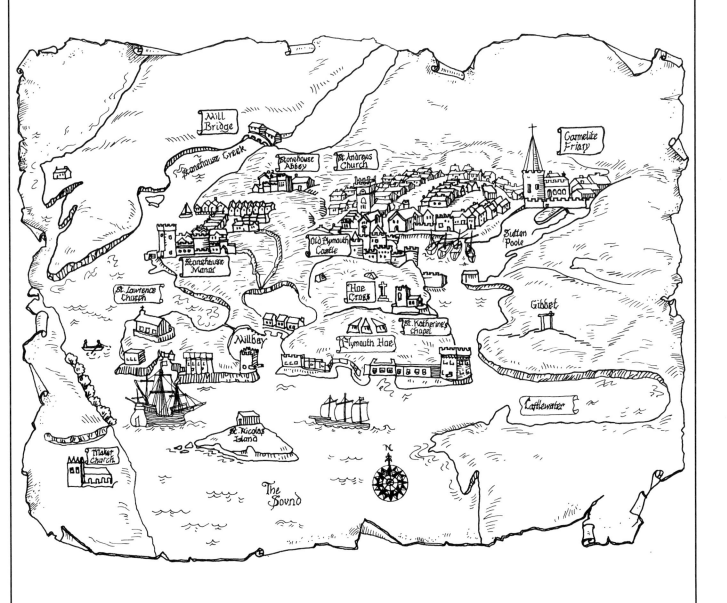

Assessment sheet

Name _____

I have used these sources to find out about life in Tudor towns:

documents and printed sources	☐	television	☐
artefacts	☐	radio	☐
pictures	☐	computer program	☐
photographs	☐	music	☐
buildings and sites	☐		

The three main differences between Tudor town life and town life today are:

1 _____

2 _____

3 _____

The following things are the same in towns today as they were in Tudor times:

_____

_____

_____

_____

Rural life

Contents

Rural life

Background information

*T*he danger of making sweeping generalisations when describing Elizabethan life applies to country life as well as to towns. Local conditions influenced both the type of crops grown and local industry.

So, once again, children will find it more relevant and helpful to concentrate on local Tudor country life – and, again, local maps are useful for this.

Most people in Tudor times lived in the country in small villages which were often made up of only a dozen or so houses. At a national level, land enclosure had affected many areas, particularly in the south. This had brought the common-field system to an end and large, village farms were split up into smaller farms. There is evidence to show that this caused much hardship and was one of the reasons for the increased number of poor people.

The same crops were grown on small and large farms as had been for centuries but increased trade with other countries meant that new crops were gradually being introduced. One of the best known was the potato, brought to England by Sir Walter Raleigh, but it is unlikely that the potato would have had any major impact on eating habits before the end of Elizabeth's reign.

Contrasting lifestyles, both regionally and in terms of wealth, make it particularly difficult to gain an overall picture of country life in Elizabethan England.

The elaborate Bradford table carpet depicts a hunt taking place in the countryside.

The local availability of building materials meant that the houses of the rich differed from one region to another, while little is known about the daily life of the very poor. It is likely that they lived in simple cottages with thatched roofs and earth floors, although there is some disagreement about whether such houses had an upstairs. There would have been little furniture and the family would have lived in one small room.

The local lord of the manor held most of the power. However, the leet court, an administrative division which originated in medieval times, continued to hear grievances and to lay down local rules and regulations. The leet court was held twice a year – during the month after Easter and during the month after Michaelmas.

The manor had its own local courts which were run by local magistrates – all of whom were principal landowners appointed by the Crown. It was particularly important for power to be localised as it meant that, when farming conditions were poor, potential trouble could be stopped at source.

Most people were farmers and so failed crops meant starvation. In December 1596 there were seven deaths from starvation in Newcastle and 25 within two months of the following year.

People who did not have their own land were in an even worse position. They would be hired out – often on a daily rate – as hedgers and ditchers, harvesters and thatchers. Shepherds and milkmaids would be paid by the year.

This painting, known as The Tichborne Dole, shows Sir Henry Tichborne, a rich landowner, in front of his new country house. He is surrounded by all the local villagers who depended on his wealth to survive.

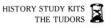

Care for the poor

Life would have been far from idyllic for the vast majority of people. Records show that the question of what should be done about the poor was as pertinent an issue as it is today. There was a distinction made between people who were seen as 'deserving of help' and those who were 'thriftless'.

Some attempt was made to help people in the first category but anyone seen as being responsible for their own poverty was punished. Sometimes this involved being sent to a House of Correction where they were made to work.

There is also evidence of bands of vagabonds moving from town to town, which partly explains the laws prohibiting the entry of foreigners to a town. If caught, these people could be branded or whipped and put into the stocks.

Travelling people were the subject of several punitive laws. In 1554, an Act was proclaimed giving gypsies 20 days to leave England. Ten years later, it was made a capital offence for anyone to consort with gypsies.

Black settlement

By the end of Elizabeth's reign, a number of Africans were living in the country. It had become fashionable to employ African servants – we know that Walter Raleigh had one. However, in 1596, Elizabeth issued orders that black people must be sent abroad and, in 1601, a Royal Proclamation stated that *'negroes and blackamoors'* should be expelled from England on the following grounds: *'great annoyance of her own liege people who want the relief which these people consume, as also for that the most of them are infidels having no understanding of Christ or his Gospel'.*

Getting dressed

Portraits of the gentry show the types of outer clothing worn by wealthy Tudors. The section covering *Court life* provides some examples of the clothing that Elizabeth owned.

It is possible to trace changes in fashion during the Tudor period as well as individual preferences. Men like William Cecil are painted in fairly sombre clothing, whereas Drake, Dudley and the Queen dressed far more elaborately.

As discussed in the section covering *Town life*, what people could wear was restricted in accordance with their status in life. Portraits of children show that they wore the same style of clothes as their parents. These garments were made at home from strong materials that would last a long time. Clothes

This detail from the Cobham portrait shows a popular fabric design – one layer of material was slashed to allow another layer to show through.

were rarely washed – and only wealthy homes would have had facilities for clothes washing. They used large wooden tubs and soap made from a mixture of fats and ashes dissolved in water (see visual resources pack).

Herbs were sometimes used to make clothes smell nice.

Women and girls

Under their outer garments, wealthy Tudor women and girls wore a chemise, which was put on first thing in the morning. This was a long garment, rather like a night-dress. In the winter it would be replaced with a flannel shift or shirt for added warmth.

Next, they would put on stockings with garters at the knee and then a corset which would have been made of leather was laced down the front and had two side pieces that stuck out over the hips.

Over this was a bodice with separate sleeves that were tied on to the bodice at the waist. Then came waist-petticoats. The top petticoat would show at the front of the gown. A piece of clothing known as a *stomacher* – a stiffened piece of material – was laced securely into the front of the bodice.

Portraits show that the gown was cut open at the front and reached to the ground. During the sixteenth century, some dresses were made in two pieces – the bodice part became the *body* and the skirt part the *kirtle*.

By the end of the century, fashionable ladies were wearing enormous hoops around their waists, known as *farthingales*. The kirtle was stretched over this. A ruff was worn around the neck of the bodice. It was stiffened on wire to make it stand out from the neck.

Ruffs became larger during the Tudor era and must have been extremely uncomfortable.

Poorer people wore softer corsets and stockings of rough, woollen material.

Hair was normally covered with a scarf or hat and wealthy women, including Elizabeth, often wore wigs.

Men and boys

Men and boys wore shirts and a fitted jacket or *doublet* to which their hose (tights) were tied by laces, called *points*. Breeches, worn over the hose, were very short and full, with the bottom edge tied up to the waist. The doublet came below the waist and had slits or slashes in the material so that the shirt could be pulled through. This effect can also be seen on some portraits of Elizabeth. It seems to have been fashionable to show one material through another of a different colour.

Both men and women wore cloaks when it was cold. At the beginning of the Tudor period, these were long enough to reach the ground but, by the end of the period, fashionable gentlemen had shortened their cloaks to waist or ankle length.

Men's and women's shoes were made of leather, satin or velvet and had low heels. Again, it was fashionable to have slashes in shoes so that the coloured lining showed through. Hats

A painting of Sir Walter Raleigh and his son sporting typical Tudor fashions, including doublet and hose.

were also often slashed and were sometimes tall and rounded with a brim and sometimes much flatter with a long feather.

Night-shirts were worn at night. Wealthy people would have had special ones and we know that Anne Boleyn had a night-shirt of black satin, lined with taffeta and edged with velvet. Less wealthy people probably slept either in their day clothes or naked but most people wore a nightcap.

When children were born, they were wrapped in swaddling bands which people believed kept the different parts of their body from drifting apart. Both boy and girl babies were dressed in petticoats and frocks which sometimes makes it difficult to tell the sex of a young child in a portrait.

Boys began to wear breeches when they were about six or seven which might be when they became more toilet trained.

Food and cooking

There is considerable evidence to tell us what wealthy people ate (see *Court life* – Background information), but it is much more difficult to find out about the diet of the majority people who left no written evidence.

As most people lived in the country, we can assume that they produced their own food and bartered or sold any surplus.

Their food would have been simple – pottage with a few vegetables and herbs, bread, cheese, whey, eggs, bacon and, occasionally, a chicken, rabbit, wild bird or fish. Snaring birds was common and even larks and blackbirds were eaten.

Most families made bread from rye and barley, although if crops failed it might be made out of peas, beans, oats and whatever else was available.

Vegetables would include onions, beans, leeks, cabbage, parsnips and turnips. Some people believed that root vegetables were unhealthy because they grew in the ground and they were seen as food of the poor. This may partly explain the high meat content of the Hampton Court diet.

A series of poor harvests resulted in famine although many people could survive a single poor harvest by eating things like ground acorns. In these circumstances, cats, dogs and rats would have been used for meat.

People rarely drank milk, using it mostly for making butter and cheese, which would be done in the home. They did not drink water either and even children were given ale to quench their thirst at meals. Beer and wine were becoming more popular with the wealthy by the end of the century.

Where it existed, tableware was made of wood or pewter. People had wooden bowls and square or round *platters* which were the earliest form of plates. Sometimes one course was eaten on one side of a platter and the next on the other side. Forks were unknown and eating was done with knives, which were pointed at the tip and had a straight cutting edge.

The invasion of the Armada introduced new foods into English homes and led cooks to invent new preservation recipes for longer voyages. In Plymouth, for example, cream was baked and bottled to send to sea while methods of curing and preserving ham and bacon varied from place to place.

Honey, salt, juniper and pine tar were used in some areas as a preservative while cheese was often wrapped in cloth to preserve its moisture.

Lesson Plan : Rural life

Objectives

Classroom based activities
1. Knowledge about population distribution in Elizabethan England and about particular aspects of Tudor country life.
2. Development of concepts related to bias, class, change, economy and evidence.
3. Skill in using secondary source material to obtain evidence about life in Tudor England.
4. Skill in using primary source material, such as inventories and surveys, to find out about life in the Elizabethan era.
5. Ability to distinguish between the lifestyles of different classes in the Tudor era and to ask historical questions using historical language.

Homework
1. Ability to use primary and secondary source material to re-create a background for a well-known fairy story.

Resources

Reference books about Tudor town and country life, costume and daily life, local county map, for example, by John Speed[15], local town map, if available, for the Tudor era[16], other locally-based written source material for the Tudor period.

Display

Then and now display, showing particular aspects of Tudor life, such as costume, in contrast to today. Display showing the different sources of evidence that the children have collected about town and country life in Tudor times.

Content

Introduction
1. Brainstorm the children's ideas about country life today. List the work done in the countryside. Explore the children's experiences of country life.
2. Compare a contemporary map of Elizabethan England with a modern map.
3. Help the children to recognise that the majority of the population lived in the country and worked on the land and in the home.

4. Record the differences between England today and in Elizabethan times, using maps.
5. Examine reference books, particularly illustrations, that show country life in Elizabethan times. Discuss the source material for these illustrations. How do we know what country life was like?
6. Record the types of activities that took place on a farm (using fact sheet A).

Development
1. Compare information collected on one aspect of Tudor life, such as clothing, with today (using fact sheets B and C).
2. Compare information collected with that for Elizabethan court life (using research sheet).

Extension activity
1. In pairs, use the information from Will's diary to discuss Will's impressions of town life comparted to life back home.

Homework activities
1. Read the story of *Town Mouse and Country Mouse*[17] and retell it in a Tudor setting.

Assessment

AT I, Level 2c – Identify differences between Elizabethan England and England today.*
AT I, Level 3a – Describe how fashions changed during the Elizabethan era.
AT I, Level 3b – Suggest reasons why people moved from the country into the towns in Tudor times.
AT I, Level 4a – Recognise that similarities and differences between classes in Elizabethan society may be reflected in similarities and differences in today's society.
AT I, Level 4c – Arrange, label and display pictures, maps and diagrams which illustrate aspects of country life in Tudor Britain.
AT I, Level 5c – Understand how the Tudor diet was likely to be influenced by the increase in sea travel.
AT 2, Level I – Understand that there were real people who lived in the Tudor era.*
AT 2, Level 2 – Understand that people living in the country might have different views about their lives than those living in the town.

* Suitable for lower ability levels

Fact sheet A

Name _____

Rural life

In Tudor times, most people lived in the country and paid rent for their house and land to the local landowner. We know from illustrations and tapestries of the period the sort of work that farming involved.

These illustrations come from a book written at the beginning of the Tudor era – but we know that very little had changed by the end of that period. We also know that even very young boys and girls worked on farms and this is still the case in many countries in the world today.

Name _____

Tudor costume

Farmer

Yeoman

Merchant

Carpenter

Merchant's wife

Shepherd

Labourer

Farmhand

Fact sheet C

Name _____

Using written sources: Costume

Here is a summary of the clothes that peasants could wear according to the law:

Doublets and breeches – plain woollen cloth with no slashing
Shirts – unbleached linen with plain collars
Hose – wool, often white
Shoes – leather
Gowns – servants' gowns might reach the leg, but were no longer than this
Caps – women had to wear caps of white woollen yarn unless it could be proved that their husbands were gentlemen

Note: *Slashing* describes clothes which were cut or slashed to allow a different coloured material beneath to show through. Clothes like this were normally worn by rich people.

Name _____

Inventories

In Tudor times, inventories were made when people died. They were a list of all the things which belonged to the dead person. Today they provide us with a good written source of evidence for what domestic life was like at that particular time.

Circle any words in the list below that you do not understand.

Use a dictionary or a reference book to find out what they mean.

Write down here any words that you still do not know.

The inventory of John Porter of Rainhill Village, July 1588

In the dwelling house:

1 iron pot, a grate and tongs	*33p*
4 brass pans and a skimmer	*30p*
7 pewter dishes and 12 spoons	*35p*
4 chairs, 3 stools, 1 form	*14p*
4 noggins, 18 trenchers, 10 saucers	*14p*
Earthenware in the house and buttery	*15p*
2 spinning wheels	*13p*
1 fall board and treen ware	*43p*

On a sheet of paper, make a list of:

i   the furniture and bedding that John Porter owned.

In the chamber in the upper end of the house:

1 feather bed, 2 chaff beds, 2 blankets, feather bolster, 2 pillows, chaff bolsters and hangings	*£1.50*
In linen	*£1*
3 chests	*30p*
3 barrels	*10p*
1 lacquered bed, 1 rug, 1 feather bed, 1 bolster, 2 pillows	*£1.50*
A plough and plough irons, a hack of iron	*£1*
Hay	*£3*
1 horse and a mare	*£6.50*
1 cow, 2 heifers and 2 calves	*£7*
2 carts and a pair of wheels	*60p*
A grind-stone and 2 troughs	*5p*
Apparel	*50p*

ii   the animals which belonged to him.

What was his most valuable asset?

Use reference books to draw as many of his possessions as you can.

Research sheet

Name _____

Class differences in Elizabethan times

In the spaces below, record any differences you have found between Elizabethan court life and life in the country:

	Elizabethan court life	**Country life**
Food		
Clothing		
Houses		
Entertainment		

Name _____

Then and now: Maps

Here is a map of England in Tudor times

Here is a map of England today

Mark the town nearest to your school on both maps.

Record three differences between the maps:

1 _____

_____

2 _____

_____

3 _____

_____

Activity sheet C

Name _____

Using illustrations: Work

What jobs are the people doing in this picture?

What time of year do you think it is? How can you tell?

What do you think the woman is carrying in the basket?

Name _____

Then and now: Washing

It is very difficult to find pictures of ordinary
life in Tudor England. This drawing is based on
an illustration found in the British Museum.

Write down two things which are different from today.

1 _____

2 _____

Write down two things which are the same.

1 _____

2 _____

Activity sheet E

Name _____

The poor

The following passage comes from a
description of England which was written in
1577 by William Harrison:

'With us the poor is commonly divided
into three sorts. Some that are poor like
the fatherless child, the aged, blind,
lame, and the diseased person that is
judged incurable; the second are poor by
casualty as the wounded soldier, the
decayed householder, and the sick
person....the third consisteth of thriftless
poor as the rioter that hath consumed
all, the vagabond that will abide
nowhere'.

In the box on the right, re-word the passage above in ordinary English.
You may find that you can leave out some words.

What does William Harrison mean by *'poor by casualty'*?

A poor because they have lost their savings?

B poor because they are sick and cannot work?

C poor because they have never worked?

What is meant by a *'vagabond that will abide nowhere'*?

_____

_____

_____

Name _____

Causes and consequences:
Why were so many people poor in 1600?

Fill in the gaps. The first one is done for you.

Cause	Consequence	Tick
In some places, common land was enclosed	*Families lost land*	
Prices were going up in the shops		
Some wounded soldiers and sailors had no one to look after them		
There were some bad harvests		
The population was growing		

Do you think that any of the causes listed above make people poor today?

Tick those which you think apply to life today.

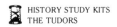

Assessment sheet

Name _____

I know three ways in which life for people in the country in Tudor times was different from life in the country today:

I _____

2 _____

3 _____

Will, from the diary story, moved to Plymouth because:

I think Will was likely to eat different food from his family because:

I have used these sources to find out about life in the Tudor countryside:

It is difficult to find source material which tells us about:

Life at sea

Contents

Life at sea

Background information

*H*ere we take the children away from domestic Tudor life to look at what was going on outside England. This involves difficult concepts - such as empire, colony, exploitation and slavery.

The children should understand that England has always been influenced by outside forces and has influenced what has gone on in other countries. These influences may not always have been for the good and stories about past heroic deeds should be examined from more than one point of view.

Sea travel was the key to expansion during the Tudor era and *Will's First Battle* provides good background information about life at sea. It also sets the political events of Elizabeth's reign in a story context.

Going to sea was no soft option. A visit to the reconstructed *Golden Hinde*[18] – Francis Drake's flagship – gives a sense of the appalling conditions with which sailors had to cope.

There is plenty of visual source material showing what Tudor ships were like but this does not tell us who went to sea and what sea life was really like. *Will's first battle* shows how one boy adapted to life at sea and the sort of work undertaken by English ships. The story of Sir Francis Drake is another good starting point as it raises important questions about trade, exploration and the growth of the Empire.

Sea trade

By the time of Elizabeth I's reign, England had been involved in overseas trade for several centuries and had been exporting wool to the Continent since the thirteenth century.

By the end of the sixteenth century, exports were becoming slightly more varied, both in terms of the goods and where they went.

However, the bulk of export trade was in wool, while imports consisted of a variety of raw materials, food and manufactured goods.

The stagnation of the traditional cloth trade meant that new trade markets had to be found.

When the country was fighting with Spain, trade with the Spanish colonies was forbidden although there is considerable evidence to show that some trade did continue.

So, ambitious merchants looked to India and China, trying to open up a western route, and set about establishing colonies in America to forge new trade links.

The only systematic records for overseas trade are the port books kept by government officials and the local customs' accounts of ports like Chester and Southampton. These show both coastal and overseas trade.

Explorers

A number of famous English sailors helped to establish new trade routes during Elizabeth's reign. The most famous were Frobisher, Gilbert, Davies, Raleigh and Drake.

The Golden Hinde – Sir Francis Drake's flagship.

The life of Sir Francis Drake

1541 or 1542 – Born near Tavistock.

1549 – Religious riots resulted in Drake's family fleeing to Plymouth. From there they went to London by sea and, for some time, lived on an old hulk at Chatham. Later, Drake's father became chaplain to the navy.

1555 – Drake went to sea on a merchant ship trading between London and Holland.

1564 – The Spanish seized all trading ships en route to Holland to stop the English helping the Dutch rebels.

1566 – Drake's first voyage to the West Indies.

1567-9 – Drake joined an expedition to the West Indies with Sir John Hawkins, a relative. Hawkins was already involved in the slave trade, from which he made his fortune. It is clear that Drake intended to follow his example.

1574 – Drake was in Ireland.

1577-80 – Drake became the first Englishman to sail around the world in his ship, the *Golden Hinde*. He returned with valuable cargo. Elizabeth benefited from his financial success and Drake was knighted the following year. Drake bought Buckland Abbey, near Plymouth, where he settled with his second wife.

1587 – Drake attacked and destroyed part of the Spanish Armada fleet in Cadiz harbour.

1588 – Defeat of the Spanish Armada. Drake was in charge of the Plymouth Squadron which played a major part in the defeat.

1595 – Drake's last voyage to the West Indies where he died and was buried at sea.

Miniature portrait of Sir Francis Drake.

Challenges

The lives of people like Sir Francis Drake raise important questions about the influence of individuals on the course of history. In a school context, such stories provide an interesting context for finding out about the past. But there are important problems to face, particularly when the story telling is done at a simplistic level with younger children.

Stories of famous characters chronicle key events but, unless there is additional and accessible information, they give only a limited picture of these individuals and the times in which they lived. Children need to develop the historical skills of enquiry and questioning that allow them to identify bias in such stories. For example, we hear little about Drake's family life. We know that he had no children and was married twice but it would be interesting to know more about the lives of these two women who must have spent a great deal of time alone managing the household while Drake was abroad.

Hawkins, who was an important influence on Drake, made his fortune from the slave trade. Some historians avoid exploring the morality here, saying that Hawkins and Drake were only products of their time. But there is no reason why the issues cannot be discussed with quite young children. Activity sheet D gives an opportunity to discuss the growth of the British Empire in terms of its impact on vanquished peoples and on the black people already living in England.

The Empire

The attempts to build up English colonies in America failed, probably because the colonists either died of disease or lack of food or because the Native Americans objected to their settlement. However, other important trading links were being established – for example, with India – which were to have important implications for the establishment of the British Empire during Victorian times.

Sir Walter Raleigh

Sir Walter Raleigh was one of the most important men in England in connection with the attempts to form colonies in America.

It is said that he met the Queen while out walking. He saw a puddle in front of her and immediately took off his new cloak and put it on the ground so that she did not have to step in the water. As a result, he became one of the Queen's closest courtiers. However, it is more likely that he became one of Elizabeth's favourites because he was introduced to her by another favourite – Robert Dudley, Earl of Leicester.

In 1583, Raleigh took the leading role in the attempts to found a colony overseas. The capital for his first adventure, to explore the coastline of what is now known as North Carolina, would have come from his own pocket. When Raleigh brought back good reports of the area, Elizabeth agreed that it should be called Virginia (The Virgin Queen) in her honour.

This first colony was set up in 1585 but it did not last long. Those people who managed to live through the harsh winter returned to England the following year.

A second colony was set up in 1587 but was found abandoned three years later.

Raleigh realised that friendship with the native Americans was vital but neither here, nor on his later expeditions to South America, was he successful in either founding a viable colony or in finding the fabled gold of 'El Dorado'. As a result, he fell out of favour with Elizabeth and was later executed by James 1.

Tudor seamen

Not all seamen were as eager to set sail as Will in the diary. Many were press-ganged into joining the navy or sailing on cargo vessels.

Exploration vessels were more attractive as the crew expected to share the profits of their voyages.

Certainly, the crew on the *Golden Hinde* did extremely well as a result of its successful navigation of the world, and returned with valuable cargo.

Conditions at sea were appalling. Henry VII and Henry VIII had begun to fit crews out in green and white uniform but Elizabeth thought this too costly. It is likely that most seamen were poorly dressed.

Hammocks had been seen in use in the West Indies but it was some time before they became an essential part of English ship life. Men slept where they could although officers had cabins and captains often had a carved wooden bedstead – Drake's was taken from a Spanish ship.

Food was kept in barrels with salt or vinegar used as preservatives. Sailors were allocated one pound of biscuits and one gallon of beer a day, one pound of salt meat four days a week and fish on three. But on long voyages food went bad and the beer turned sour so men often starved. Lack of vegetables produced scurvy, which made gums swell, teeth fall out and blue swellings appear on the legs.

Cooking made the ship hot and this made it even harder to keep food fresh. On his

Food on board ship during Tudor times was basic and included biscuits like this one from the later date of 1884

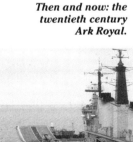

Then and now: the twentieth century Ark Royal.

A seaman climbs the rigging on a reconstruction of the Golden Hinde.

voyages, Drake took only enough food and water to last until the ship reached West Africa where he could get fresh produce.

On larger ships, officers might get a few delicacies – such as figs, raisins, walnuts, almonds and olives.

Rats would have been rife on board ship and were probably eaten when conditions became very bad.

Pirates

There were many pirates at sea during Tudor times. However, the definition of piracy depended on who was doing what to whom. Drake's attacks on the Spaniards in South America were really acts of piracy but he was knighted when he returned to England with a valuable cargo.

The navy was too small and busy to deal with pirates and, as many leading citizens had shares in pirate ships, it is unlikely that much would happen to them if they were caught.

Ships

During Elizabeth's reign, there was a permanent navy of about 30 ships with names such as Vanguard, Ark Royal and Elizabeth Jonas.

Activity sheet A shows a picture of the *Ark Royal* taken from a sixteenth-century woodcut. This was the flag-ship of the fleet which defeated the Spanish Armada.

The biggest navy vessels had to be specially built and merchant ships were also used for battle.

Lesson Plan : Life at sea

Objectives

Classroom based activities
1. Knowledge about famous explorers, growth of the Empire and trade, and life on board ship.
2. Development of concepts of anachronism, bias, colony, cause, evidence, government, hero, motive, myth.
3. Ability to follow and understand historical fiction.
4. Skill in interpreting historical fiction as a source of evidence about the past.
5. Skill in interpreting bias in factual stories about the past.
6. Ability to use primary and secondary source material to find out about life at sea and the reasons for voyages of discovery.

Homework
1. Using reference and information-finding skills to find out more about particular explorers or voyages.
2. Communicating basic ideas about the lives of different groups of people in Elizabethan times.

Resources

Will's diary, illustrations and portraits showing a variety of Tudor ships, contemporary maps of the known world, portraits of explorers.

Display

Maps of the world with voyages of English ships marked. Contemporary map of the world. Portraits of Drake and Raleigh. Pictures of English ships.

Content

Introduction
1. Read aloud, or let the children read, Will's diary either at one sitting or over a period of days. Children should have plenty of time to discuss the story and identify historical content, such as: life on board ship; the work of a merchant ship; Drake's role in the Armada defeat.
2. Tell the life story of Sir Francis Drake and compare it with Will's story. Identify how the stories differ as historical source material.

Development
1. Draw, write, act or re-tell Will's story.
2. Use maps and reference books

to find out why Drake was keen to establish an English colony in America.

Extension activities
1. List the historical facts in Will's diary. Write down what might have happened next.

Homework activities
1. Use reference books and maps to find out about two other Elizabethan explorers or to find more detail about Drake's voyage around the world.
2. Compare the lives of an Elizabethan town dweller, a country woman and a seaman.

Assessment

AT I, **Level 1a** – Place in sequence events in Will's diary. *
AT I, **Level 2b** – Suggest reasons why Thomas thrashed Will. *
AT I, **Level 2c** – Identify differences between explorers in the past and explorers today.
AT I, **Level 3b** – Suggest reasons why Drake was keen to establish an English colony in America.
AT I, **Level 4a** – Identify which elements of a seaman's life are the same today as they were in the past. Identify some things which have changed.
AT I, **Level 4b** – Suggest more than one way in which Elizabethan seamen could meet their death.
AT I, **Level 4c** – Act in a drama where three Elizabethans meet – someone who lives in a town, someone who lives in the country and someone who goes to sea. Discuss the different lifestyles.
AT I, **Level 5a** – Distinguish between what happened to Will as a result of his experiences on board ship and the changes in the work of the merchant ship he was on.
AT I, **Level 5b** – Suggest some social consequences of poor living conditions on board ship, both short- and long-term.
AT I, **Level 5c** – Write an account of Drake's voyage around the world, linking different aspects – political, economic, scientific.

* Suitable for lower ability levels

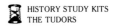

Fact sheet A

Name _____

The Golden Hinde

This is an illustration of the **Golden Hinde** – the ship in which Sir Francis Drake went around the world.

The map below shows the route he took. The journey took three years and cost four ships and many seamen's lives.

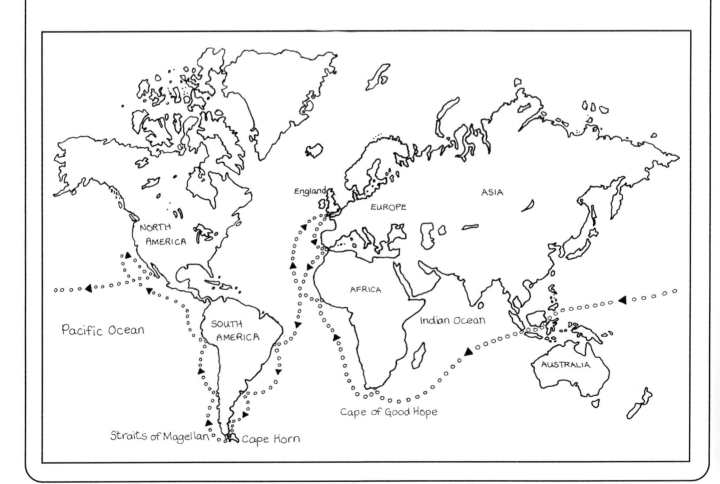

Name _____

Trade routes

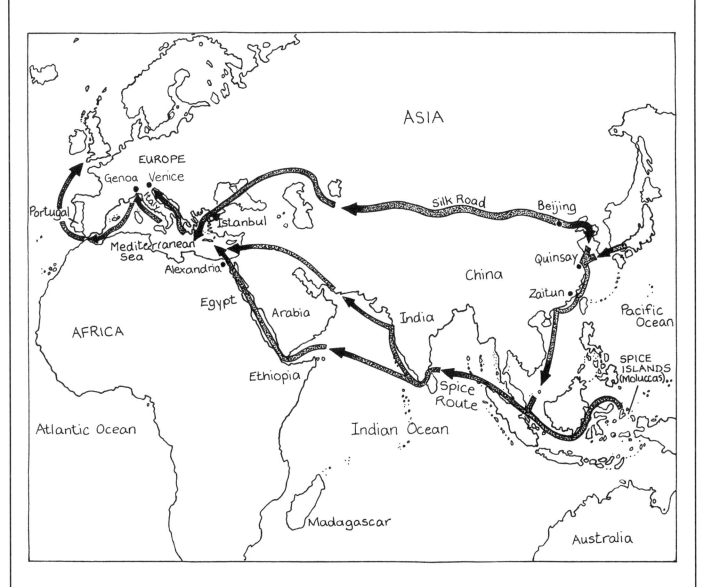

It was difficult to keep food fresh in Tudor times and spices were used to flavour food so that it tasted better. But spices were very expensive, so only rich people would have been able to afford them. This meant that merchants wanted to trade in spices so that they could make money. This map shows the traditional routes that merchants from England would have had to take to get their spices. When these routes were closed down in the middle of the Elizabethan era, the merchants were keen to find other ways of reaching the east.

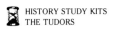

Fact sheet C

Name _____

Tudor ships

These are some of the different types of ships
used in Tudor times:

Fishing vessel

Merchant ship

Galleon

Name _____

Now and then: The Ark Royal

Then

Now

What is the same about these two pictures?

What is different?

Activity sheet B

Using sources: The slave trade

Name _____

Source A

'Hawkins then did business with the citizens.
He sold them 150 negroes and cloth and
linens in exchange for gold, pearls and silver.
He sent the governor 60 negroes in exchange
for the 400 pesos which had been given him
from the King's chest'
Statement of Robert Barrett (1568)

What evidence do sources A and B provide
about John Hawkins?

Source B
This is John Hawkins' crest.

Source C

'The first Englishman to line his pockets by
trafficking in black slaves was an
unscrupulous adventurer called John
Hawkins....He acquired 300 inhabitants of
the Guinea coast....He took these people to
the Caribbean island of Hispaniola where
he sold them to the Spaniards for £10,000
worth of pearls, hides, sugar and ginger....
Elizabeth lent Hawkins, for his second slave-
hunting voyage, the Jesus of Lubeck.'
***Staying Power* by Peter Fryer (1984)**

Why does Peter Fryer (Source C) call John
Hawkins an 'unscrupulous adventurer'?

Is Peter Fryer's description of John Hawkins
a fact or an opinion?

Who might disagree with Peter Fryer?

Find out what the Jesus of Lubeck was.

Name _____

Virginia

This illustration shows what Virginia (North Carolina) seemed like to the English during Tudor times.

What information about America does the picture give us?

Does the picture make you want to visit America?

What dangers or bad points does the map not show?

Using court records

'Report of the goods washed ashore between Liverpool and Crosby from the small ship belonging to Thomas Knype. Report made in 1594 for the Admiralty Court, found with the manuscripts of the Earl of Derby at the Lancashire Record Office.'

Hamper: felt, velvet, ruffs, taffeta, a doublet, 43 hat bands.

Portmanteau: shirt, 3 collars, 3 ruffle bands, a handkerchief, 7 knives, a purse with £11.50, a purse with 68p.

Hamper: 40 treen (wooden) cups, 9 small dishes, 22 knives, 9 pairs of spurs, 5 sword hilts, 4 pommels, 32 sword handles, 132 wool cards.

Chest: cloth breeches, cloak, 24 pens and ink-horns, 4 rolls of silk, 25 pieces of fustian, 36 wool coloured stockings, 12 wool garters, a roll of shot silk, 12 girdles, 10 pieces of lace, 216 silver buttons, 72 gold buttons, 576 silk buttons, 576 copper buttons, 7 pieces of velvet lace, a piece of silk lace, 12 pairs of gloves, 24 perfumed gloves, 12 fine gloves, lace, 2 lengths of embroidered garters, a paper of black silk, a paper of coloured silk, 12 silk purses, a remnant of Milan fustian, 24 children's purses, 24 small look-glasses, 6 broken look-glasses, 48 small purses, 12 fine knives, 22 sword blades, 132 knives, 24 silk tassels for knives.

Bundle: 26 wooden bottles, 2 bags of nails, 1 lantern, 1 copper pan.

Hamper: 74 treen cups, 1 bent ladle, 14 sword handles, 132 wool cards, a bag of hops worth nothing and thrown onto the dung hill.

Goods found at Liverpool: 24 spurs, 24 flat locks, 10 round locks, 24 treen cups, 56 earthen cups, a small bag of brass.

On the reverse of this sheet, put the goods listed in the passage into the following categories:

clothing

materials

cutlery

crockery

others.

What do the contents of the chest tell us about how some people lived in Tudor times?

No one from the shipwreck survived and we do not know why the boat sunk. Suggest two reasons why. Do you have any evidence?

1 _____

2 _____

Name _____

Food on board a Tudor ship

Barrels were used for storing food.
Here is a list of some of the most common
food found on Tudor ships:

*salt beef, butter biscuit, salt fish, cheese, beans,
bacon, dried peas.*

Salt or vinegar would be used to preserve the
food.

What sort of food is missing from this list to
form a healthy diet?

Scurvy was a common disease at this time. It
killed more English seamen than enemy guns
did. Use a reference book to find out what
causes scurvy and what were the symptoms.

Look at the illustration above, then suggest
some problems about cooking and eating
below decks.

Assessment sheet

Name _____

Portraits and illustrations of Tudor ships show:

Spices were needed in Tudor times because:

Drake was keen to establish an English colony in America because:

Elizabeth I gave money to men like Drake because:

Religion

Contents

Religion

Background information

*R*eligion was an important factor in people's lives in the Tudor period. Everyone went to church which, at the beginning of the era, meant the Catholic Church. By the time Elizabeth died, this had changed.

How much the religious changes affected the majority of people is difficult to say. In some areas, such as Lancashire, religious change was probably fairly minimal. In others, nearer to London, ordinary people would have been affected more closely by the political and ideological issues involved.

These issues were extremely complex and are still argued over by historians today. For the majority of primary children, an overview is all that is needed but this will vary according to the children's age, ability, interests and experiences. Teachers in Catholic schools may find that the break with Rome has more relevance to their children than it would to others.

Contemporary illustrations like the one below symbolised Henry VIII's attempts to control the power of the Pope and the Catholic Church in England.

The section on *The Monarchy* includes a brief outline of key events relating to the monarchy. This may be enough detail for younger and less able primary children. This section, however, looks in greater detail at the key political events which were linked to the break with Rome.

Henry VII passed on to his son, Henry VIII, a strong kingdom whose subjects had a temporal allegiance to him and a spiritual allegiance to the Pope in Rome. However, in Europe the first rumblings of the Protestant Reformation were beginning to be heard.

In the early years of his reign, Henry VIII relied heavily on his father's councillors but their influence lessened with the rise of a man called Thomas Wolsey (above left), who became Lord Chancellor in 1515. Basically, Wolsey ruled the country while Henry spent time enjoying himself – for *'Twenty years of hunting, feasting and loving'* as one book says.

Relationships with France

Henry VIII was keen to gain a reputation as a military commander. For this and other reasons, England joined the Holy League against France. The Holy League of 1511 was organised by Pope Julius II and was directed against the growth of French power in Italy.

In 1512, Spain, Venice, the Holy Roman Empire, Switzerland and England came together in an anti-French coalition and the French were driven out of Milan.

When the French tried to return in 1513, they were defeated at the Battle of Novara.

After this, the allies could not agree on strategies and started to make separate agreements with France.

England and France made peace and, in accordance with the peace treaty, Henry's younger sister, Mary, married the King of France, who died soon afterwards. Mary later remarried and one of her grand-daughters was Lady Jane Grey, who was made queen for nine days after the death of Edward VI.

In 1520, Henry and Francis I of France met in France for what can only be described as a sixteenth-century version of a summit conference. Known as the *Field of the Cloth of*

Gold (see visual resources pack), it was a massive show of glory where the two kings and their courtiers spent four weeks enjoying banquets, jousts and feasting.

The break with Rome

In 1521, Henry produced a book which criticised the writings and teachings of the growing Protestant faith. For this he was awarded the title *Defender of the Faith* by the Pope, Leo X. However, this close relationship between the King and the Pope was soon shattered by a complex series of events.

1 The need for a legitimate male heir

Henry already had an illegitimate son but he desperately needed a legitimate heir. By the mid 1520s, this was beginning to look impossible. By then his existing wife, Catherine of Aragon, was in her forties and had had numerous miscarriages and still-births. Henry wanted to take a new wife – Anne Boleyn. He hoped that the Pope would declare his marriage to Catherine null and void, on the grounds that she had been married to his brother, and would give his blessing to Henry's marriage to Anne.

2 Political changes in Europe

If circumstances had been different a marriage annulment might have been possible but, by 1527, the political climate had changed and the Pope was at the mercy of the Spanish King, Charles V, who was Catherine's nephew.

3 Failure to solve the divorce question through an English Court

Wolsey's attempts to hold a court in London to hear the case for annulment failed and this signalled the end of Wolsey's power.

4 Henry becomes Supreme Head of the Church of England

To subvert the Pope's power in England and to enable Henry to marry Anne Boleyn, the King was declared the Supreme Head of the Church of England. He later married Anne Boleyn who gave birth to Elizabeth not long afterwards. To ensure the loyalty of all his subjects, Henry demanded that they take an Oath of Supremacy which confirmed that Henry, not the Pope, was Head of the English Church. Two leading statesmen, Sir Thomas More and John Fisher, refused to take this oath and were eventually executed.

5 Growth of Protestantism

The Protestant Reformation was a growing force in Europe and a number of Henry's advisers were sympathetic. At this stage, the new Church of England was little different from the Catholic religion but there were powerful influences that ensured that the seeds of the Protestant Reformation took strong roots in England.

6 Pragmatism of leading Protestant reformers

The destruction of papal authority was no doubt seen by many Protestants as the first step towards the purification of the Church. They strongly supported a more independent approach to religion but moved slowly, making use of the differences between Henry and the Pope. By 1536, the publication of the *Ten Articles* defined the doctrinal position of the Church of England.

7 Dissolution of the monasteries

People had been criticising the wealth of the Church for some time and the King needed money. The dissolution of the monasteries supplied him with the necessary funds and he rewarded those faithful to him with lands confiscated from the Church.

8 The English Bible

A bible was written in English which was open to individual interpretation – an important element of the Protestant Reformation.

9 Changing alliances

The truce between France and Spain forced Henry to seek an alliance with Protestant countries. This was reflected by his fourth marriage to Anne of Cleves.

10 The accession of Edward VI

Edward's advisers were strong Protestants and worked to ensure that England remained a Protestant state. Two English prayer books were issued, one in 1549 and one in 1552, and the churches and services were simplified.

Edward VI

Mary I saw it as her duty to return England to the Catholic faith.

A change in direction

The attempt to place the Protestant Lady Jane Grey on the throne after Edward died resulted in disaster. The people of England disliked the political manoeuvring behind Lady Jane Grey's nomination and supported Mary as the rightful heir even though they recognised that her accession to the throne would bring a change in religious and political direction. Mary was a strong Catholic and saw it as her duty to return England to the Catholic fold.

At first, this was done gradually and foreign reformers were encouraged to leave the country and ministers were appointed to devise ways of restoring the Catholic faith. These advisers speeded up the process of change. Between 1555 and 1558, about 300 men and women were burned for heresy, even though most of these people had little power with which to threaten Mary's Church.

These deaths, together with Mary's marriage to Philip of Spain, probably served to advance the Protestant cause more than anything else.

Mary's marriage was disastrous both for her personally and for England politically. It was never a popular marriage and led to war with France as Spain's ally. This resulted in the loss of Calais, which had been England's last possession in France.

Mary died in 1558, leaving the throne to her Protestant half-sister Elizabeth.

Elizabeth I and Rome

Protestant bishops Latimer and Ridley being burned at the stake during the reign of Mary I.

Finding some form of religious settlement was one of Elizabeth's most urgent problems and, to satisfy the vast majority of people, she worked hard to establish an open Church. However, Elizabeth is quoted as having said that she had no desire to 'open windows in men's souls'.

At the start of her reign, as long as people attended church on a Sunday that was enough. Private masses were ignored.

But this had to change when, in 1570, the Pope issued a bill deposing the Queen and absolving her subjects from their allegiance to her. As a result, practising Catholics were turned into potential traitors and so were persecuted.

Elizabeth and marriage

Like Mary, Elizabeth's choice of husband was seen as a key issue but, unlike Mary, she played her cards extremely carefully.

Her advisers saw a husband not only as the potential father of the heir to the throne but also as the man likely to rule the country. His political allegiances would be of paramount importance. Elizabeth spent several years of her reign in discussions with suitors but remained single.

Mary Queen of Scots

When Elizabeth came to the throne, her cousin Mary ruled Scotland. Fact sheet D shows how the two women were related.

Mary was not popular – partly because she was a Catholic ruling a Protestant country and partly because she had become involved in a series of political intrigues involving her husband, the Earl of Bothwell, and Lord Darnley, the man she later married.

Mary was forced to abdicate in favour of her son James and fled to England in 1568.

Mary was a great problem for Elizabeth. She was a queen and Elizabeth was keen to make sure that she was treated as such but, once in England, Mary provided a focus for leading Catholics. So, Elizabeth began to have her guarded like a prisoner, putting her in the care of George Talbot, Earl of Shrewsbury and husband to Bess of Hardwick. At first, Mary's life with the couple was quite pleasant and it is still possible to see some of the embroidery on which she worked there at Hardwick Hall (see Places to Visit in the Teachers' notes). However, later she was given less freedom.

Immediately after Mary's arrival in England there was a rebellion in her favour led by the Earls of Northumberland and Westmorland which aimed to restore Catholicism and place Mary on the throne.

The rebellion was put down but there was then a series of other conspiracies, often involving foreign powers.

Eventually, Mary was executed. The break with Rome now seemed final – but the battle for people's souls rumbled on during the seventeenth century.

Lesson Plan : Religion

Objectives

Classroom based activities
1. Knowledge about the break with Rome.
2. Understanding of the importance of religion in Tudor England.
3. Development of ideas about the effects of religious intolerance.
4. Development of concepts – authority, bishop, Catholic, change, cause, evidence, Protestant, reaction, religion.
5. Understanding of chronology related to changes in religious beliefs.
6. Skills in using and analysing evidence.

Homework
1. Skill in preparing and asking historical questions.
2. Ability to record information gained in an interview.

Resources

Bible, prayer book, religious books from other faiths.

Display

Pictures and photographs showing a variety of different religious buildings, including as many faiths as possible, timeline showing changes in religion, linked to monarchs, map showing religious allegiances during Elizabeth's reign.

Content

Introduction
1. Find out who goes to church, to a mosque or to another place of worship. What happens there and what does it mean to them?
2. Look at local religious buildings in the area. Record different ones.
3. Look at a diagram of the interior of a church.
4. Link these aspects with school assemblies and the messages they give about different faiths.
5. Examine the idea that England today is multi-faith and tolerant of the religious beliefs which people hold. Contrast this with the views about religion at the start of the Tudor period. Use contemporary examples to show the effects of religious intolerance today.
6. If there is a house with priest holes near to the school, use this

as a way of showing how Catholics were treated during Elizabeth's reign (activity sheet F).
7. Examine the role of religion in England today.

Development
1. Construct a timeline to show changes in religion. Use reference books to find out what happened under different Tudor monarchs.
2. Work through activity sheet D and record information about the break with Rome.

Extension activities
1. Use reference books to find out about Mary Queen of Scots and the reasons why she was executed.

Homework activities
1. Interview a friend or relative about what religion means to them in their everyday lives.
2. Record three things which show how religion today is different from religion in Tudor times.

Assessment

AT I, Level 2b – Suggest one reason why Henry VIII broke with Rome.
AT I, Level 2c – Identify one way in which religion is different today than it was in Tudor England.
AT I, Level 3a – Record the different religions of the Tudor monarchs.
AT I, Level 3b – Suggest one reason why Mary Queen of Scots was executed.
AT I, Level 3c – Talk about or record the differences in religion during Henry VII's reign and Elizabeth's reign.
AT I, Level 4b – Examine a priest's hole in a book, or at a site, and suggest more than one reason why such holes were built into houses.
AT I, Level 5a – Distinguish between the closure of the monasteries as a religious change and their closure as a social change.
AT I, Level 5b – Record some political and social causes and consequences of the dissolution of the monasteries.
AT I, Level 5c – Show how Henry VIII's need for money was linked to the dissolution of the monasteries.
AT 2, Level 5 – Discuss how a film such as *A Man for All Seasons* may show a different perspective on the break with Rome.
AT 3, Level I – Talk about different sorts of religious buildings. *
AT 3, Level 3 – Recognise that the cover from the first Bible printed in English indicates a change in the way Christianity was taught in England.
AT 3, Level 4 – Use several different historical sources to record the differences between the interior of a church in Henry VII's reign and one in Elizabeth's reign.

* Suitable for lower ability levels

Fact sheet A

Name _____

Timeline

Henry VII

1485–1509   Catholic

Henry VIII

1509–1547	Catholic at the beginning of his reign.
1521	Awarded title *Defender of the Faith* by the Pope.
1534	Act of Supremacy made the monarch, rather than the Pope, Head of the English Church.
1535	The first printed English Bible.
1536	The dissolution of the monasteries began.

Edward VI

1547–1553	Protestant Heavily influenced by Protestant reformists.
1549	The first English prayer book.

Mary I

1553–1558   Catholic
Attempted to restore England as a Catholic country.

Elizabeth I

1558–1603   Protestant
In 1570 was excommunicated and deposed by the Pope. Took stern measures against Catholics.

Name _____

Places of worship

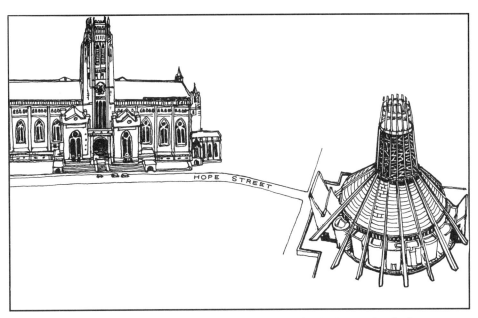

Anglican cathedral   Catholic cathedral

Temple

Salvation Army Hall

Mosque

Synagogue

Fact sheet C

Name _____

Parts of a church

A church is made in the shape of a cross on
which Jesus was crucified. The body of the
church is called the **nave**, the **transepts** are
the arms, and the **altar** is the head of the cross
in which the choir and sanctuary are found.

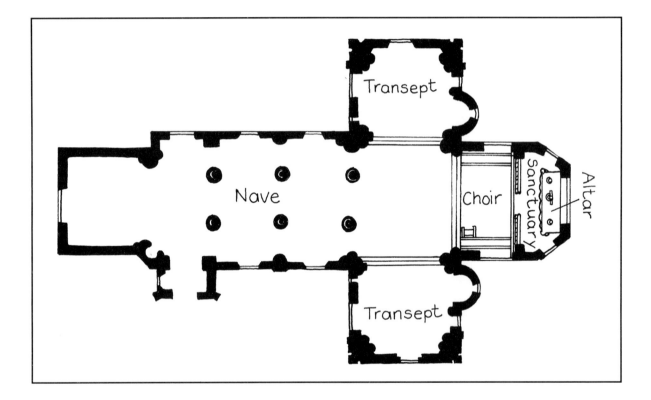

Name _____

Church interiors before and after the break with Rome

Before the break with Rome

After the break with Rome

What can you see that is the same in these two pictures?

What can you see that is different?

Activity sheet B

Name _____

Evidence of different religions in our community

Write down the names of as many different religions as you can in five minutes.

Write down three things that you know about one of these religions.

1 _____

2 _____

3 _____

Draw a building that is linked with one of these religions.

Draw two artefacts that are linked with this religion.

Name _____

Title page of the Coverdale Bible, 1535

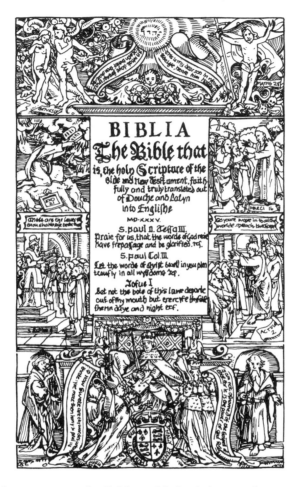

This is an illustration of the front cover of a Bible published during the reign of Henry VIII.

Look at the picture carefully.

Can you find:

1   Adam and Eve
2   Christ risen from the dead
3   Moses receiving the Ten Commandments
4   Christ sending the Apostles into the World
5   St Peter preaching to the Jews
6   Henry VIII?

Why do you think the artist put Henry on the front of this Bible?

Activity sheet D

Name _____

The break with Rome

The break with Rome was illustrated in art at the time. The illustration below shows the four evangelists[*], Matthew, Mark, Luke and John, stoning the Pope. It comes from a painting done in 1540.

Why do you think that the artist made this painting and what was he trying to say?

How has the artist tried to show that God is on the side of the evangelists?

[*] **Evangelist** is the name given to the men who wrote the Gospels in the Bible.

 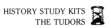

Name _____

The dissolution of the monasteries: True or False?

Use reference books to try to find out if the following statements are true or false.
Remember that sometimes we just do not know the answer.

	True	False	Don't know
All monasteries were rich.			
Henry made a lot of money from the dissolution of the monasteries.			
Sir Francis Drake lived in a house that had once been an abbey.			
Some monasteries survived.			
Monasteries and convents were shelters for the poor.			

Do you think Henry VIII was right to close down the monasteries?

Name _____

Priest holes

Source A
After 1570, Catholics were persecuted.
    They were heavily fined if they did not attend church.
    Parents were not allowed to send children abroad for a Catholic education.
    Catholic priests were declared traitors. A special group of priest hunters was formed.

Use these three sources along with some reference books to answer these questions:

1   Why did Elizabeth start to persecute Catholics after 1570?

Source B
Wealthy Catholic families, such as the Norris Family of Speke near Liverpool, had priest holes built into their houses. If anyone came to the house the priest could be hidden away.

2   In what way was life made difficult for anyone who wanted to be a Catholic?

Source C

3   What evidence do we have that Catholic masses continued?

Name _____

Family Tree: Mary Queen of Scots

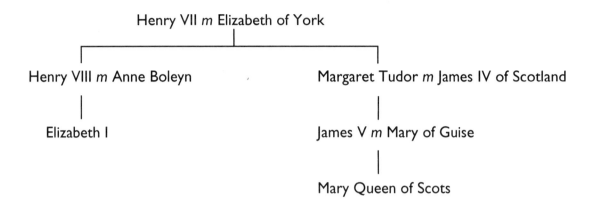

Henry VII *m* Elizabeth of York

Henry VIII *m* Anne Boleyn

Elizabeth I

Margaret Tudor *m* James IV of Scotland

James V *m* Mary of Guise

Mary Queen of Scots

m = married

MARIA
D G
SCOTIA
PIISSIMA REGINA
FRANCIA DOTARIA

"I should be Queen of England because…"

Mary Queen of Scots

E R

"I should be Queen of England because…"

Elizabeth I

Assessment sheet

Name _____

The Catholic faith is no longer the official religion in England today.
This is because of the following events which took place during Tudor times:

The word **intolerance** means:

Religious intolerance was shown in Tudor times by the following people:

The dissolution of the monasteries meant that:

I have used these sources of evidence to find out about religion in Tudor times:

Travel

Contents

Travel

Background information

Maps and map-makers

Comparing travel and transport in Tudor times with that of today provides an ideal opportunity for teachers to draw on children's environmental awareness. In many ways, this is a particularly suitable topic for younger juniors and less able children as it allows them to use their knowledge and experience to make simple comparisons with the past.

Historical maps provide good written and visual sources of evidence. Christopher Saxton made the earliest printed maps that we have of the 52 English counties. They were originally published in 1579, as a result of Saxton's travels around the country over a period of seven years. John Speed's maps were published about 30 years later and drew on Saxton's work. Speed also drew up 73 town plans which were the first real records of what Tudor towns were like.

Map of Northamptonshire created by Christopher Saxton, 1576.

Children can compare these county maps with modern regional maps, noting any motorways, roads, rail and canal systems. Speed's maps do not show main roads although they do mark rivers. It is not known why Speed omitted roads. He may have thought that the information was not worth including or that travellers would have their own road guide. In spite of this, these early maps provide a picture of what the country looked like and are an ideal starting point for non-readers.

The map on Fact sheet A shows the main roads and navigable rivers in England in 1600. This is secondary, rather than primary source material, and is derived from maps made at the time, such as those of Speed and Saxton. It provides some information about the means of communication.

Fact sheet B provides an example of an Elizabethan map made at the time of the Armada. This has been simplified and much greater detail is available on county maps.

We know a reasonable amount about travelling conditions because there were a number of men – and even a few women – who travelled the country and wrote down what they saw. Some people made records for personal use while others, such as John Norden, were asked to '*travel through England and Wales to make more perfect descriptions and charts*'. They travelled on horseback and made notes on buildings, customs and what people were saying and doing.

Roads

No one had made roads since Roman times – the word *road* was used to describe the right to pass from place to place rather than a thoroughfare. Even at the start of Elizabeth's reign, there was no real policy for roads, except that people who owned manors were required to cut down trees and undergrowth for 200 feet on either side of the highway from one market town to another and to fill in any ditches.

However, in 1555, an act was passed requiring each parish to elect someone to be responsible for maintaining the roads for one year. This involved able-bodied men doing four days' labour a year. This made little difference as the roads were still being described as 'noisom and tedious' by the end of the century. There were no milestones or signposts, so the wealthy long distance traveller had to employ a guide.

Elizabeth I would travel short journeys on a litter.

Goods transport

Goods were usually carried on pack-horses because horses could go where carts could not. As road journeys were often dangerous, people tended to travel together and avoided travelling after dark.

Often, merchants and their pack-horses would travel together in a long line called a *pack-horse train*. The horses had panniers hung on either side for carrying goods. Sometimes they were used for carrying young children. The pack-horse carriers would also take letters and messages from place to place and brought plenty of news with them about the things they had seen and heard on their journey.

Horses could be hired at inns and public houses – names such as *The Packhorse* and *The Woolpack* provide evidence of this.

Royal couriers provided the fastest form of transport and this service improved considerably during the Tudor period. For example, when Henry VIII died it took six days for the news to reach Scotland from Greenwich. When Elizabeth died, it took half that time.

However, passing news to and from Ireland continued to be difficult because of the sea crossing – a regular packet boat was not established until 1599.

Private transport

Most long-distance road travel was done either on horseback or in vehicles pulled by horses.

At the start of the Tudor period, the only type of private carriage was a wagon without springs but coaches were introduced towards the middle of the century. Activity sheet B shows how one clerk reacted when he saw one of these for the first time. Early coaches were fairly uncomfortable and made passengers feel sick as they swung them to and fro.

It is not surprising that Elizabeth preferred to travel on horseback.

Poor people travelled about very little and when they did it would have been on foot or in wagons. These *stage-wagons* were heavy carts pulled by eight or ten horses.

They were so named because journeys were made in stages, each of about 12 miles. They travelled at about two miles an hour and had no seats.

Passengers sat on the floor among straw or on bales of any soft goods that the wagon might be carrying. It is unlikely that people travelled unless they had to!

The Queen's progress

There are several portraits showing Elizabeth travelling. A litter would be used for short journeys – a favourite subject for portrait painters as it enabled them to paint the Queen in all her glory.

Travelling on a litter also became part of an elaborate public relations exercise for it enabled people to see their Queen.

This sense of ceremony still exists today when members of the royal family use stage-coaches on special occasions.

Most summers, Elizabeth I left London for a progress through part of the country.

She never went far from London, never north of Stafford or west of Bristol, and never abroad.

The court would move with her and it might take as many as 400 six-horse wagons to carry all their goods because the court had to bring its own furniture and stores.

There is plenty of evidence to show that extensive preparations took place at both ends of the journey to ensure that everything ran smoothly.

Children can compare how today's royal family travels with the transport used in Tudor times.

As soon as news was received of the Queen's intended arrival in a town, work was started on the roads, which would be covered with gravel.

The floor of any house she might enter would be swept and covered with fresh rushes and herbs, entertainment would be prepared and the town cleaned up.

Elizabeth visited her own palaces but also liked to stay with leading courtiers. For her hosts, the cost of the Queen's visits must have been enormous but the possibility of advancement if the visit went well would have made it worthwhile.

Rivers

Heavy and bulky goods could be transported much more economically by water than by land. Grain, coal, iron and building materials were carried as near to their final destinations as possible by water.

Inland towns, such as York and Norwich, became river port towns as well as market towns.

However, many rivers were beginning to silt up and became difficult to navigate. A few small canals were built but little money was invested in improving water transport at this stage.

Sea travel

Will's diary shows that trade and travel with Europe was fairly common in Tudor times.

Small ships, such as the one on which Will worked, would cross and re-cross the Channel, mainly carrying wool from England and returning with wine, timber and pottery.

A delftware wine bottle – this type of pottery was very popular during Tudor times.

By the end of the Elizabethan era, trading posts had also been established in America and Africa and, in 1601, Elizabeth signed a charter establishing the English East India Company.

Trade was also carried out around the coasts of England and Wales, for example, coal was transported by sea between Newcastle and London and corn was taken from Pembrokeshire to Bristol and North Wales.

Even this local coastal trade could be dangerous. For example, court records found with the manuscripts of the Earl of Derby at the Lancashire Record Office show that in 1594 a small ship or 'bark' belonging to a Liverpool merchant called Thomas, was shipwrecked between Liverpool and Southport. The contents found provide an interesting dimension on the sort of trade between local ports and listed below are some of the items found in a chest. It is thought that these goods were probably on their way between Chester and Bristol:

'cloth breeches, cloak, 24 pens and inkhorns, 4 rolls of silk, 25 pieces of fustion, 36 wood coloured stockings, 12 wool stockings, 2 silk girdles, 3 remnants of linen cloth, a roll of shot silk, 36 French garters, 216 silver buttons, 72 gold buttons, 576 silk buttons, 7 pieces of velvet lace, a piece of silk lace, 12 pairs of gloves, 24 perfumed gloves, 12 fine gloves, 2 lengths of embroidered garters, a paper of black silk, a paper of coloured silk, 12 silk purses, a remnant of Milan fustion, 24 children's purses, 24 small look-glasses, 6 broken looking-glasses, 48 small purses, 12 fine knives, 22 sword blades, 132 knives, 24 silk tassels for knives.'

A typical Tudor merchant ship.

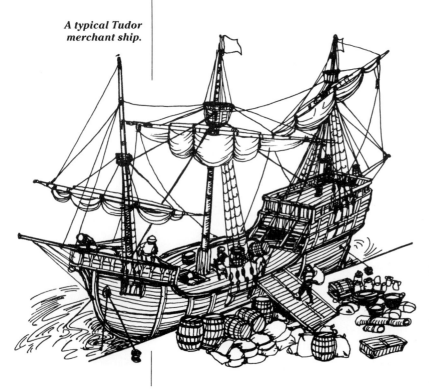

Lesson Plan : Travel

Objectives

Classroom based activities
1. Knowledge about different forms of transport in Tudor times – road, sea and river.
2. Development of concepts related to change, evidence, modern, primary and secondary sources.
3. Ability to work with maps as secondary and primary historical source material.
4. Skills in chronology.
5. Skills in questioning historical source material.

Homework
1. Developing skills of chronology.

Resources

Individual county maps, maps of Tudor England, primary or secondary, pictures and illustrations of different forms of Tudor transport, reference books.

Display

Portrait of Elizabeth I in procession, map from the visual sources pack of England and Wales at the time of the Armada.

Content

Introduction
1. Discuss and record the different ways in which children travel to school today. Record other forms of road transport.
2. Look at a local map or plan showing roads and/or motorways near to the school.
3. Look at a local county map drawn during the Tudor period. Discuss: the way in which the map-maker has shown different parts of the county; place names which pupils recognise; spellings which have changed; the sort of countryside it is showing; what the map tells us about the past in this county. Discuss the differences between the county then and now and explore the reasons for this. Compare it with a modern map, discussing the map style, symbols and roads.

Development
1. Use reference books to find pictures or illustrations of how people travelled in Tudor times.
2. Present a visual record of the different forms of transport in the past and today.

Extension activities
1. Look at the variety of forms of transport available today, such as road, sea, air and rail transport.
2. Record some advantages of travel today compared with Tudor times.

Homework activities
1. Use reference books about the history of transport to create a timeline showing examples of road travel from four different periods, starting with Tudor times and finishing with present day.

Assessment

AT 1, Level 2b – Suggest why people in the past travelled by foot or by horse.
AT 1, Level 2c – Record the differences between road travel now and in Tudor times.
AT 1, Level 3b – Give reasons why road transport is easier today than in Tudor times.
AT 1, Level 4c – Look at primary map sources and describe different aspects of the Tudor countryside.
AT 1, Level 5c – Discuss the reasons why travellers wanted to travel in groups rather than by themselves.
AT 1, Level 6a – Recognise that some aspects of road travel today may not be as pleasant as in Tudor times.
AT 2, Level 1 – Recognise that the different forms of transport shown in pictures and illustrations really did exist. *
AT 3, Level 1 – Talk about the portrait of Elizabeth in procession. *
AT 3, Level 2 – Recognise that the portrait provides us with information about how the Queen travelled. *
AT 3, Level 3 – Discuss some of the advantages and disadvantages of travelling on a litter.
AT 3, Level 4 – Use information from maps, illustrations and portraits to describe transport in Tudor times.

* Suitable for lower ability levels

Fact sheet A

Name _____

England's main roads and navigable rivers around 1600

Name _____

England in 1588

Fact sheet C

Name _____

Different forms of road transport in use in Tudor times

Name _____

Now and then: Road transport

Now   **In Tudor times**

What other forms of transport did not exist in Tudor times?

Activity sheet B

A new invention

Report of the visit of the Earl of Derby to Liverpool, 1566:

'My lord the Earl of Derby then being brought to this town in a (............................), with ii great horses nobly addressed and iiii yeomen all in green attending on foot.'

This extract comes from the Liverpool Town Books.

How do you think the Earl of Derby travelled to Liverpool?

Did you notice that the Clerk has used Roman numerals? How often are these kind of numbers used today?

How many horses did he have? How many yeomen?

Why do you think the clerk left a gap in the record?

Name _____

Elizabeth in procession

Where do you think Elizabeth might be going?

What advantages would the Queen have travelling in this litter?

What disadvantages would there be?

Use reference books to find out about and draw other sorts of carriages used in Tudor times.

Activity sheet D

Name _____

Buildings as evidence

What evidence about the past do these public house signs give us?

What other public house signs give us evidence about the past?

Name _____

A tour of England

'I have travelled in your dominions both by the sea coasts and in the middle parts, sparing neither labour nor costs.....There is almost neither cape nor bay, haven, creek nor pier, river or confluence of rivers, beaches, washes, lakes, meres, fenny waters, mountains, valleys, moors, heaths, forests, woods, cities boroughs, castles, principal manor places, monasteries and colleges, but I have seen them.'

A man called John Leyland wrote these words in the late 1530s. He had spent six years touring England.

To which Tudor monarch do you think he was writing? What was he saying?

How do you think he travelled?

Why did it take him so long?

Why do you think he went on such a journey?

Assessment sheet

Name _____

I know that travel was different in Tudor times because:

I have used the following sources to provide evidence for this information:

Maps made in Tudor times show:

Travel by road today has problems because:

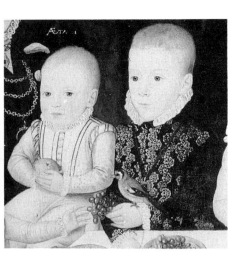

Children

Contents

Children

Background information

*T*he best way for children to understand what it was like to be a child in Tudor times is to use their experience of childhood today.

Less able and younger children can look at particular aspects of their childhood, such as school life, and compare them to the Tudor period, while older juniors should be developing a more general awareness of Tudor life of which childhood is just one element.

This involves exploring the difficult question of relationships between adults and children. It may help to set a study of Tudor childhood within a wider development education project which explores issues such as child labour and the status of children in communities throughout the world.

Will's first battle provides an opportunity for teachers to explore further children's relationships with parents and other adults in Tudor times.

Working children

Will Martin would have been typical of many Tudor children who came from working families. He had left his home in the country to live and work in his uncle's house in Plymouth.

Will Martin, the central character from Will's first battle *is typical of many Tudor children who had to go out to work at an early age.*

The opening lines of the diary tell us that his own family lived on a farm, where conditions were poor and starvation was a great threat. Will would use his wages to help his family. Before he left for Plymouth, Will worked on the farm. There is plenty of evidence to show that boys and girls worked hard in the fields from an early age.

One writer tells us that children were particularly useful during sowing time because they could be *'armed with a sling or with bowe, to skare away pidgen, the rooke and the crowe'*.

In towns, boys would have taken up apprenticeships at much the same age as Will, and girls would continue to work in the home or be sent elsewhere to earn some money.

Apprenticeships lasted for seven years and there were strict rules about the number of apprentices that a master could take.

Education

The work that children do today takes place in school and this is enforced by law. In the Tudor period, no such law existed and the vast majority of children received little or no schooling at all.

Most girls would learn to sew, spin, cook and run a house alongside their mothers. Girls from wealthy homes would receive some education and women in the royal circle were very well educated.

Elizabeth I had a governess, Kate Ashley, from whom she had lessons in mathematics, history, geography, sewing, dancing, deportment and riding.

She learned the principles of architecture and astronomy, French, Italian, Spanish, Flemish and even some Welsh. By the time she became Queen, she was better educated than many of the men in her court.

Several teachers were needed in big households so that children could be taught a variety of subjects and skills, such as singing.

The level of literacy in Tudor times is often assessed by the number of people able to write their own names rather than make their mark on legal documents such as petitions.

From this evidence it appears that, in the countryside at the start of Elizabeth I's reign, the majority of yeomen were illiterate but, by the end of her reign, the majority were literate.

This raises some interesting questions about the provision of formal education. Clearly, local and parish schools must have been achieving quite good results.

Many people who could read and write learned to do so in their parish schools. Thomas Hobbes, the philosopher, *'went to schoole in Westport church'* from the age of

In Elizabethan times, schoolchildren read from books made from animal horn, like this one.

four to eight. In most areas, there was probably one elementary school for every one or two parishes.

Literacy rates were lower among women than men but many girls did attend village schools and a few grammar schools are known to have taken girls.

The majority of girls from wealthy families would have been taught at home by relatives or tutors.

During Elizabeth's reign, several schools were founded for boys. So, boys whose fathers were wealthy went to grammar school when they were seven or eight years old.

Before they went, they had to know how to read and write in English and this would be learned at home or at schools known as ABC schools.

Here children learned the alphabet and the Lord's Prayer from a horn-book, which looked rather like a wooden bat. The letters and words were written or printed on a piece of paper which was then stuck on to the bat and a thin piece of horn fixed over it to stop the letters from wearing away. As the horn was transparent, it was possible to see the writing underneath.

Children from wealthy families might have a horn-book at home. The alphabet was learned in the form of 'A for Apple pie' and so on. After the horn book, children went on to simple reading books.

They were taught to count with a counting frame which had rows of coloured beads arranged in tens.

There was no distinction between grammar schools and public schools. The public schools all started as grammar schools, serving each neighbourhood. A few schools, such as Winchester and Eton, allowed children to live in as boarders and many grammar schools made provision for poor boys to be taught for no payment.

Standards of entry varied and popular schools often raised their entry requirements.

Parents had to provide books and candles in the winter.

The school day was long, starting at 6 am and sometimes going on until 6 pm. There would be breaks for prayers, breakfast and lunch.

Every grammar school had a single authorised grammar textbook and children learned by rote.

The teaching of written Latin was a high priority and most grammar schools taught this subject alone. Some schools taught Greek, and a few taught Hebrew.

English literature was not studied and history was covered by two poems written in Latin – *The battles of the English* and *The reign of Elizabeth*.

There were a few globes and maps but no regular geography lessons. Arithmetic took the form of accountancy.

Children wrote with a goose-quill pen which had to be sharpened with a penknife. Ink was kept in an ink-horn. Good quality paper was expensive, so heavy emphasis was placed on neat presentation. Accurate copying was another essential skill.

Control of schoolteachers was introduced in 1556, when a synod forbade anyone to

Stratford Grammar School in Warwickshire is one of a number of English schools that date back to Tudor times.

This contemporary illustration shows a Tudor classroom in 1592.

and peddlers sold simple toys at fairs held regularly in most towns.

There were very few books, so children would learn stories by hearing them told by adults.

Bible stories formed an important part of this oral tradition, as did fairy stories such as *Jack the Giant Killer*, *Tom Thumb* and *Beauty and the Beast*.

Nursery rhymes were also popular and versions of *Sing a Song of Sixpence*, *Three Blind Mice* and *Mary, Mary Quite Contrary* all existed.

Outdoor games, such as hop-scotch and blind man's buff, were well established by Tudor times and there is both written and pictorial evidence of other activities, such as wrestling, stoolball, 'pitching the bar', football, tops, battledore – a game played with a racket rather like shuttlecock – leapfrog, see-saw and bowling the hoop.

Children – particularly boys – were treated as miniature adults, so they were also involved in many adult leisure activities such as archery, sword play, fishing, falconry and hunting.

Clothing

Children wore the same style of clothing as their parents and young boys wore dresses until they were ready to be *breeched*.

At one stage in Elizabeth's rather turbulent childhood, a request was put in for more clothes for the princess. This provides an interesting list of the clothes that a young princess might be expected to have:

'She hath neither gown,
nor kirtle, nor petticoat,
nor kerchiefs, nor rails
(undergowns), *nor body
stitchets* (corsets), *nor
sleeves, nor mufflers,
nor biggens* (soft boots)'.

teach until they were examined and licensed by a bishop.

A few illustrations exist of Tudor schools. They show that punishment, or threat of punishment, played an important part in school life.

Some pictures show children being beaten with birches which were about two feet long and looked like the birch brooms which are sometimes used for sweeping up leaves.

Children were also punished by being hit on the hand with a *ferula*, a flat length of wood like a ruler with a round piece at one end.

Children could stay in the grammar school until they were 18 but the majority left well before that. Some started apprenticeships in their early teens. A few went up to Oxford or Cambridge, which were the only two universities in England at the time.

Leisure

Paintings and illustrations from Tudor times give us some clues about the different types of games children played and the toys they had.

Evidence of toys comes from the homes of the wealthy. Some babies are shown holding rattles and girls are shown holding dolls which are clothed in dresses exactly like their own.

Toys would have been hand-made, either by someone in the household or brought from abroad. Much of the early professional toy making was done in Germany.

Ben Johnson, writing in 1614, mentions hobby-horses, gingerbread figures, miniature animals, dolls, fiddles and drums – all being sold in Bartholomew Fair. Hawkers

Lesson Plan : Children

Objectives

Classroom based activities
1. Knowledge about different aspects of childhood in Tudor England.
2. Ability to compare school life today with that of a Tudor child.
3. Development of concepts related to bias, change, continuity, evidence, class, cause and law.
4. Ability to work with illustrations as a means of extracting evidence about Tudor schooling.
5. Ability to use historical portraits to find out about Tudor childhood and bias in evidence.
6. Skill in extracting information from written source material.
7. Skills in chronology.
8. Skill in asking historical questions.

Homework
1. Skills in referencing and information finding.

Resources

Illustrations of Tudor school room (activity sheet A), horn-book (provided), nineteenth-century written source (activity sheet E), reference books, Will's diary.

Display

Pie-charts showing comparisons between the day of a pupil in a Tudor grammar school and in a primary school today.

Content

Introduction
1. Discuss and/or record events in a typical day of a child today. This should include activities at home as well as at school.
2. Draw your own classroom and compare this with an illustration of a Tudor classroom.
3. Look at the illustration of a Tudor schoolroom (on activity sheet A) and record the information which can be drawn from the illustration. A similar activity can be carried out with the illustration of the horn-book.
4. Discuss questions of bias in making assumptions about schooling in Tudor times from looking at just one illustration. Record what evidence the illustration provides.

5. Record, pictorially or graphically, the differences between a school day today and in Tudor times.

Development
1. Imagine that a Tudor child is transported to the present day.
2. Record what sort of activities they would find most surprising.

Extension activities
1. Use portraits and illustrations of Tudor children to find out more about how they dressed.
2. Decide what other questions could be asked about the life of children in the Tudor period.

Homework activities
1. Use reference books to find the answers to some of your questions.

Assessment

AT 1, Level 1b – Explain why they have made particular statements about what it would be like to live in Tudor England.
AT 1, Level 2b – Suggest reasons why the school master might be beating the child in the picture.
AT 1, Level 2c – Identify differences between their classroom and that shown in the illustration.
AT 1, Level 3b – Suggest reasons why grammar schools taught Latin.
AT 1, Level 4a – Recognise that there are some things happening today that also happened in the Tudor schools - for example, learning the ABC, learning to read.
AT 1, Level 4c – Describe the different activities that a Tudor child might have undertaken.
AT 1, Level 5c – Relate why a child like Will in the diary would not be attending school.
AT 2, Level 1 – Understand that the children in the portraits lived a long time ago.
AT 2, Level 3 – Recognise that a statement such as 'The children in the picture were naughty' is a point of view, while the statement 'The picture shows one child being beaten' is a fact.
AT 3, Level 1 – Talk about what they see in an illustration of a Tudor schoolroom. *
AT 3, Level 2 – Recognise that portraits and illustrations of children in the Tudor period can tell us more about how they lived.
AT 3, Level 3 – Make simple deductions about different social groups or classes from the way they dressed and about the lack of evidence for other groups.
AT 3, Level 4 – Use information from different historical sources to make a display about children in the Tudor period.
AT 3, Level 5 – Comment on the usefulness of particular reference books in relation to the information they provide about children in the Tudor period.

* Suitable for lower ability levels

Fact sheet A

Name _____

Children in Tudor times

Here are some pictures of children in Tudor times. Some of the illustrations have been taken from portraits. They tell us about the sort of clothes that children wore and the sort of toys they played with.

Name _____

Working children

Many children worked in Tudor times. Here
are some pictures of children working.

Activity sheet A

Name _____

Inside the schoolroom

This illustration shows a schoolroom in 1592.

Find the following in the picture:
● the two schoolmasters
● pupils waiting to read
● a pupil being beaten
● a pupil writing with a quill pen and ink
● evidence that music was taught

Write down two things that are the same as in your classroom:

1 _____

2 _____

Write down two things that are different:

1 _____

2 _____

Name _____

Learning to read

This is an illustration of a Tudor **horn-book**
which was used to teach children to read.

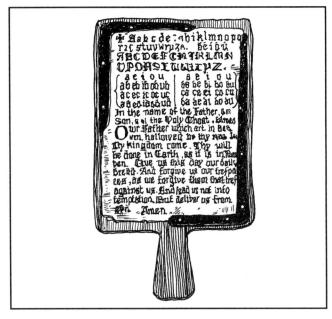

What is written on this horn-book?

Why do you think the edges of the writing are damaged?

Use reference books about writing and printing to help you to find out why Tudor children were
unlikely to learn to read using printed books.

Look at the illustration of the Tudor schoolroom on activity sheet A.
What sort of books are the children holding?

What evidence does this provide about the school shown?

Draw your own horn-book in the space provided.

Activity sheet C

Name ______________________________

Learning to write

This is an extract from a letter written by Elizabeth to her brother Edward when she was ten years old.

Qua quidem de re hoc loco satis. Illud tantum
precor ut Deus conservet tuam Maiestatem quam diutissime incolumem ad
nominis sui gloriam regnique utilitatem. Hatfildiae 2 februarii

Maiestatis tuae humillima soror
et serva Elizabeth

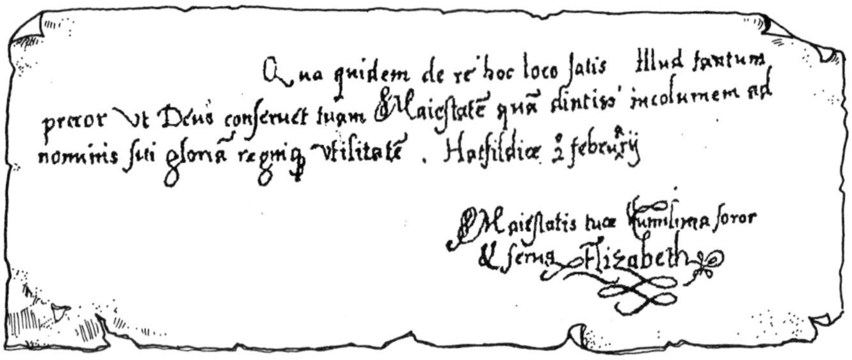

What language do you think this letter is written in?

Can you find out how old Edward would have been when this letter was written?

What evidence does this letter give about his education?

What sort of pen would Elizabeth have used?

Can you find the date on the letter extract?

Name _____

Writing and spelling

Written sources from Tudor times are very
difficult to read. Here is a short extract. The
same words in modern writing are provided
underneath, and then the same words are
provided again but with modern spelling.

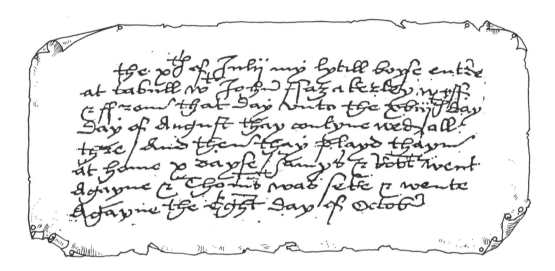

The x th of Julii mu lytill boyse entre
at tabull w. th John Ffazakerley wyff
& ffrom that day unto the xviii th day
day of August thay contynewed all
there/ And then thay playd thayn
at home x dayse / James & Robt went
agayne & Thoms was seke &
wente agayne the eght day of Octobr

The 10th of July my little boys enter
at table with John Fazakerley's wife
and from that day until the 12th day
day of August they continued all
there. And then they played them
at home 10 days. James and Robert went
again and was sick and went
again the eighth day of October.

Activity sheet D

Name _____

Building a new school

This extract comes from a book written 200 years ago. It gives us information about schools in Elizabeth's reign.

'*The Free Grammar School in Blackburn was founded by Queen Elizabeth, on the humble petition, as well of the inhabitants of the Village and Parish of Blackburn, as of other persons resident in the neighbourhood, "for the Education, Management and Instruction of Children and Youths, in Grammar" and to be called "**The Free Grammar School of Queen Elizabeth**, in Blackburn, in the County of Lancaster". To consist of one Master and one Usher.*'

What subject was to be taught in the school?

Who was to be employed in the school?

Use the words in bold to translate some of the Latin words on the school logo.

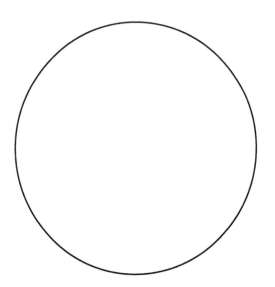

Create a logo or badge for a new school built today.

Name _____

Written source material: School timetable

Translate this passage into everyday English. It comes from the same school in Blackburn that was mentioned on activity sheet D.

'After the ringinge.....of a bell, if that can bee haid soone after six of the clocke in the mornings....there shall have prayres. After prayres they shall begine to teach at or beefore seaven of the clocke and shall continue until eleven. And in the afternoones they shall begine to teach at or beefore one of the clocke, continewinge till after fyve of the clocke, and shall than alsoe have and use prayers.

The Authors in Lattin for any introducktion may bee the grammar, Cato de Moribus, Supistris, Verulanus, Esopes Fables etc. In poetrie Terence, Ovide, Vergill, Horrace, Juvenal and Persius. In histories Salust, Cecars Comentaries, and Tullus Liuias Decades.

The Authors in Greeke may bee Cambdene or Clemades Gramar, Basills, Homer....and the Greeke Testament.

In Hebrue if any bee willinge and fitt there unto some Hebrue Gramar of Spaalter.

The principles of Arithmeticke, Geometrie, and Cosmographie with some introducktion into the sphere are proffitable.

The exersises may bee Englishes, speakinge Lattin, varicacions duble translacions, disputacions, verses, epistells, themes and declamacions in Latin and Greeke.'

Activity sheet F

Name _____

Using illustrations

These two illustrations are taken from
portraits of the same girl, Arabella Stuart. In
picture A she is just two years old. In picture B
she is 13.

Picture A

Picture B

What jewellery is Arabella wearing in picture A?

What jewellery is she wearing in picture B?

What does picture A tell you about what she liked to do?

What does picture B tell you about her interests?

What sort of education do you think Arabella Stuart had?

Name _____

Education for girls

Girls did not go to school in Tudor times. Instead, their mothers would teach them how to sew, spin, cook and run a house.

They would learn how to make butter and cheese and brew medicines from herbs.

Very wealthy families had governesses.

We know that Elizabeth I could speak French, Italian, Spanish, Flemish and Welsh. She also learned mathematics, history, geography, sewing, dancing, riding and how to behave - a subject known as **deportment**.

Why do you think that there were no grammar schools for girls in Tudor times?

What subjects do you learn today that Elizabeth did not?

Why do you think that it was important for rich people to learn foreign languages in Tudor times?

Assessment sheet

Name _____

I have used these sources to find out about life for children in Tudor times:

Tudor portraits of children give us information about:

It is difficult to get information about:

The Armada

Contents

The Armada

Background information

A cautionary note

The key historical event in *Will's first battle* is the Spanish Armada. In many ways, the story of the Armada is a wonderful example of how historical fact and fiction have become intertwined.

In 1988, the 400th anniversary of the defeat of the Armada was commemorated and this raised two important issues.

First was the whole question about the way in which such events are commemorated.

It is important for even the youngest primary children to have some understanding about the complexities of war and the suffering caused to all involved.

Events such as the defeat of the Spanish Armada cannot be reduced to a jingoistic story-telling session celebrating the victory of good over evil. History teaching has failed if children emerge with such a simplistic view.

Nor can war be seen as an activity carried out only by young men. We need to widen the perspective and show that even those who do not fight are still involved in warfare. Women, like Will's aunt, were often left at home with the sole responsibility of running a house or a trade.

The second question raised concerns the defeat of the Spanish Armada.

Traditionally, children have been taught that this was a victory for religious and political liberty over cruelty and oppression and that it was an example of the nation's courage in the face of danger. They are also taught that it was a turning point in England's rise to greatness as the world's leading maritime power.

The Armada exhibition at the National Maritime Museum in 1988 questioned this view.

It was argued that, if children were to be taught to think historically they would need to question the evidence presented to them, distinguish fact from opinion and identify bias.

This involved examining the Spaniards' point of view as well as the English and looking at a wide variety of source material.

Will's diary will help primary children to come to some understanding about the fears of those involved in a sea battle.

Older and more able children can also explore other issues. They can discuss how wars involve boredom as well as action, and why Will and his shipmates were largely ignorant of the reasons for the Spanish invasion.

While on leave in Plymouth (6 April), Will is searched by English soldiers and writes that he is more frightened of these soldiers than of the Spanish.

Europe at the time of the Armada

In the Tudor era, Europe was dominated by Spain, as is shown by the map in **Figure 1** of Europe at the time of the Spanish Armada.

Ireland was a constant source of difficulty to the Tudor monarchs. When Henry VII came to the throne only the *Pale*, a small area around Dublin, was under the direct control of a royal Deputy. We also know that at least one pretender to the English throne received support from Ireland.

A sixteenth century oil painting of the English and Spanish fleets engaged in what is thought to be the Battle of Gravelines.

Figure 1

During Henry VIII's reign, and more particularly during Edward VI's, the relationship between England and Ireland altered radically because of the break with Rome. Ireland remained only nominally under English control and the real battleground for power lay between Irish family interests.

During Elizabeth's reign, huge amounts of money were spent on supporting English settlers in Ireland.

At the same time, Philip of Spain was sending money to help those fighting against them.

Religion was used as a rallying cry by both sides and the complexities involved in this issue remain with us today.

The Portuguese had a huge Empire but, by Elizabeth's reign, this had largely been annexed and subjugated.

France was dealing with internal conflicts and had close ties with Scotland, despite differences in religion.

The Netherlands, as the map shows, were in constant revolt against Spain between 1567 and 1609 but, by the time of the Armada, the Spanish Duke of Parma had been able to

Philip of Spain

establish important bases there, despite help given by Elizabeth to Protestant rebels. In 1587, the Spanish fleet controlled the Mediterranean, the Atlantic and the Pacific.

Closer to war

When Elizabeth came to the throne in 1558, Philip II was King of Spain. This was the same Philip who had been married to her half-sister Mary and who had, in effect, been King of England until Elizabeth came to the throne.

Philip offered to marry Elizabeth but she refused and, during the next 20 years, Philip watched as she dismissed suitor after suitor.

Differences in religion were a key issue in the breakdown of peaceful relationships between the two countries but the growth of English overseas traffic must also have played a large part.

Men like Drake and Hawkins were making a living out of raids on Spanish ships and colonies and were tacitly supported in this by Elizabeth.

The execution of Mary Queen of Scots must have seemed to Philip the final straw in the persecution of Catholics in England.

It is impossible to know exactly why Philip started his *Enterprise of England*. What is certain is that it resulted in a fleet of ships being sent to England as an invasion force – known as the *Armada*.

The intention was that the Armada would sail up the English Channel and that any sea battles, together with the eventual land invasion, would be fought by Spanish soldiers based in the Netherlands and commanded by the Duke of Parma.

While the fleet was being prepared, Drake, at the head of an English fleet, sailed into Cadiz harbour and destroyed most of Philip's vessels.

A second fleet of ships was prepared and, in May 1588, set sail from Lisbon under the leadership of the Duke of Medina Sidonia. But the Spanish ships were delayed by storms and had to put into Corunna where they stayed for one month gathering new supplies and making repairs to the ships.

As a result, the Armada did not reach the English Channel until July.

When they finally arrived, beacons were lit on hilltops to carry the news across England.

The English fleet, commanded by Lord Howard, Francis Drake and John Hawkins, put out to sea from Plymouth.

Will's first battle tells the story of the Armada from Will's point of view, stationed on one of the ships which had been taken over by Drake.

While the Armada was anchored off Calais, English fireships were sent in, forcing the

The story of Sir Francis Drake playing bowls when the Armada was first sighted has been a popular theme in paintings like this one which dates from Victorian times.

Spanish to cut their anchors and drift into the open sea. The scattered boats, moving particularly slowly because of the large number of troops on board, were much easier to attack.

So, the day after it left Calais, the Armada was attacked at Gravelines and a number of vessels were badly damaged.

The Duke of Medina Sidonia recorded that he decided to lead his own ships out to meet the English in the battle at Gravelines because he was afraid that, otherwise, the whole Armada fleet would be driven onto the sandbanks at Dunkirk.

However, the Spanish suffered heavy losses and, although he wanted to go into battle once again, the Duke of Medina Sidonia realised that he was in a hopeless position. He could not retreat by returning through the English Channel and his ships were in danger of being blown ashore so, to save the fleet, he turned his ships into the North Sea to sail around the north of Scotland and return home that way. Storms hit the fleet again and more than 25 Spanish ships were wrecked on or near the coast of Ireland. It has been estimated that more than 4,000 men drowned and 2,000 reached the shore alive. Of these, some 1,500 were executed by the English. In all, between 10,000 and 20,000 of the 24,000 or more men who sailed from Corunna in 1588 died during or after the Armada campaign.

One of the commemorative medals which were made to celebrate England's victory over the Armada.

Armada evidence

Wreck objects

The gentlemen adventurers who sailed with the Spanish fleet carried modest amounts of wealth with them in the form of coins, gold chains, jewellery and silverware.

Some of these were washed up at the time from shipwrecks, while modern day treasure hunters still search for the rest.

Artefacts from wrecks such as the *Girona*, found in 1968 near Giant's Causeway in Northern Ireland, provide some evidence of life on board ship and the wealth and social status of those who drowned.

Many of these artefacts can be seen in the Ulster Museum (see Places to Visit, page 34).

Written sources

We have a number of accounts of the Armada written at the time, providing different points of view.

Contemporary maps of the route of the Armada provide additional evidence about how map makers of the time portrayed the country in which they lived.

Myths and stories

These form an important oral tradition and are a valuable historical source as they may have a basis in fact.

Oral histories of the west of Ireland, for example, have helped historians to locate the sites of some Armada wrecks.

One of the most famous stories is that of Drake playing bowls on Plymouth Hoe. He was said to be in the middle of a game when he was told that the Spanish fleet had been seen. He continued to play, confident that he had time to win the game and beat the Spaniards.

Paintings, illustrations and carvings all show this same, questionable story.

The Spanish defeat

Whether the defeat of the Spanish Armada made any difference to the imperial fortunes of England and Spain is debatable.

It showed that the English had been unable to defeat the Spanish in their own waters and that England was vulnerable to invasion.

English naval supremacy was at least 100 years away and no English Empire was created as a result of the defeat of the Armada, except in Ireland.

A commemorative medal was struck to celebrate the defeat of the *Invincible Armada* bearing the words *'God blew and they were scattered'*.

This is probably a far more realistic view of the events than is given by many of the later myths attached to the defeat.

Much of this evidence is pictorial. For example, a series of playing cards produced in the next century celebrates the victory and provides evidence about the types of ships and the events that took place.

The Armada portrait of Elizabeth included in the visual resource pack provides a wonderful example of a montage, where different images representing the Queen's power are put together to create a picture.

Lesson Plan : The Armada

Objectives

Classroom based activities
1. Basic facts about events of the Spanish Armada.
2. An understanding of what it might have been like to have been on board an English ship at that time.
3. Development of concepts related to bias, Catholic, Protestant, crusade, cause, evidence, motive, myth, propaganda, war.
4. Skill in the use of primary and secondary source material to develop concepts about war and myth and to develop knowledge of life on board ship.

Homework
1. Presenting evidence to express a particular point of view.

Resources

Reference books, map of Europe at time of Armada, portraits of Elizabeth and Philip, Will's diary.

Display

Armada portrait. Collage of boats/sailors/soldiers/families.

Content

Introduction
1. Examine war as a concept. Record the children's understanding of it and their knowledge of wars today.
2. Discuss the problems of finding out what is going on today, when information may contain bias and propaganda.
3. Play the game of Chinese Whispers to show how information can be distorted when repeated.
4. Create a timeline for the Armada based on Will's Diary. Compare it with the timeline on fact sheet A, recording known events.
5. Use role play to explore different points of view – Elizabeth/Philip, Spanish sailor/English sailor, Uncle Edward/Will.

Development
1. Use information gathered and primary and secondary source material to create a picture collage of various of the Armada.

Extension activities
1. Examine the Armada portrait and record ways in which the artist shows Elizabeth's power.

Homework activities
1. Make a write-up of the Armada for a tabloid newspaper. Take one particular episode, for example the Battle of Gravelines, and describe it, or provide an overview of the whole event. The newspaper can be Spanish or English.

Assessment

AT I, Level 1a – Place the events of the Armada in sequence. *
AT I, Level 2b – Suggest reasons why Philip of Spain wanted to attack England.
AT I, Level 2c – Identify differences in warfare today and in Tudor times.
AT I, Level 3b – Select one reason why the Armada was not invincible.
AT I, Level 3c – Identify differences between naval warfare in the Second World War and in Tudor times.
AT I, Level 4b – Suggest more than one cause and consequence for the defeat of the Spanish Armada.
AT I, Level 4c – Create a montage showing different aspects of the Armada including the experiences of people left at home.
AT I, Level 5b – Suggest some political and social causes and consequences of the Spanish Armada.
AT I, Level 5c – Show that the life of Drake symbolised some of the changes that were taking place in the world and how some of the actions of men like him contributed to Philip's *Enterprise of England*.
AT I, Level 6b – Discuss the importance that can be attached to political, social and economic causes for the Spanish action.
AT 2, Level 1 – Recognise that an event like the defeat of the Spanish Armada really happened.*
AT 2, Level 2 – Show an understanding that Philip's view of England would be different from that of Elizabeth's.
AT 2, Level 3 – Distinguish between facts about the English command of the invasion and opinions about the importance of the Armada.
AT 2, Level 4 – Show that lack of evidence about daily life means that it is difficult to find out about how the majority of the English population felt about the Armada at the time.
AT 2, Level 5 – Recognise that known information about the Armada needs to be separated from the myths which have been created about it.
AT 2, Level 6 – Show how partial selections of source material can lead to different interpretations of past events like the Armada.
AT 3, Level 1 – Talk about an illustration of a galleon. *
AT 3, Level 2 – Recognise that artefacts found from shipwrecks can tell us about life on board ship. *
AT 3, Level 3 – Make simple deductions about the Spanish retreat from looking at pictures of the ships.

* Suitable for lower ability levels

Fact sheet A

Name _____

Timeline of the Armada

This timeline shows the route taken by the
Armada through the English Channel.

1558

29 July	Armada sighted from the Lizard near Land's End.
30 July	Armada approaches Plymouth. The English fleet sails out of Plymouth.
31 July	Battle near Plymouth.
1 August	The battle of Portland Bill near Weymouth.
3-4 August	The two fleets meet in battle near the Isle of Wight.
4-6 August	The voyage to Calais.
7 August	The English launch a fireship attack on the Spanish.
8 August	Battle off Gravelines. The remaining Armada ships sail up into the North Sea, chased by the English.

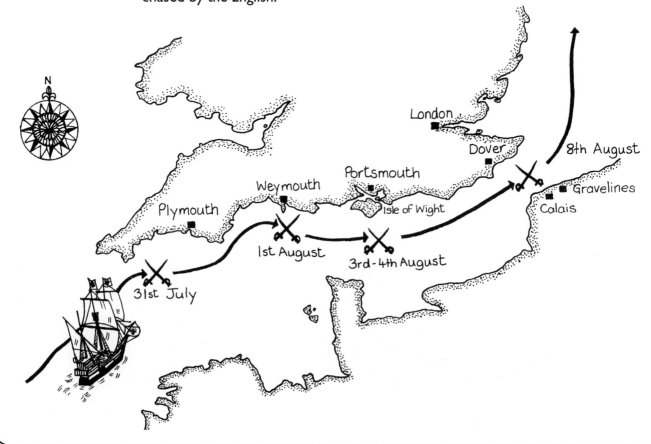

Name _____

Life on board an English fighting ship in the sixteenth century

This drawing is based on work done by staff at the National Maritime Museum in London. No proper plan of a sixteenth-century ship exists, so they have used historical sources to make a reconstruction.

Fact sheet C

Name _____

The Armada portrait

This illustration is based on a picture of Elizabeth I painted after the Armada. It is thought to have belonged to Sir Francis Drake. The picture is a colourful collage showing how powerful the Queen was. The crown is on a table by her right hand and she has her hand on a globe. In her other hand, she seems to be holding a fan. Behind Elizabeth are two windows which show different views. On the left, are the English fireships which were launched against the Armada. On the right, you can see ships rolling about in rough sea.

Elizabeth posed only about eight times for portraits and patterns were made from these sittings. A painter had to have permission from the Government before using one of these patterns. This is one reason why Elizabeth's face looks very similar in all the portraits.

Name _____

From an Armada wreck?

Put a cross on the objects that would not have
come from the wrecked Armada ship shown in
the picture below.

Activity sheet B

Name _____

Different points of view

If Elizabeth I and Philip II of Spain were
interviewed on television, what do you think
they would say about the Armada?
Fill in the speech bubbles.

Name _____

Using written sources:
A letter from Philip of Spain

> 'We are going to do God's work and we can rely on his help, unless by our sins we anger him. You will take good care that nothing is done to offend him. Above all, there must be no swearing or blasphemy. You must punish offenders most severely, lest God should punish us all.'

This was written by Philip of Spain to the Duke of Medina Sidonia who was in charge of the Armada.

Who did Philip think was going to help the Spaniards win the war against the English?

What might stop this help?

What sort of punishment do you think the men would be given?
Use Will's diary to help you.

How will God punish the Armada?

Activity sheet D

Name _____

Using written sources: the *Revenge*

This extract comes from Drake's original order
for ammunitions and weapons for his ship the
Revenge.

Powder	5000
Shott of all sorts	500
Musketts	72
Longe pikes	40
Short pikes	20
Partizannts guilte	19
Holberts guilte	20
Borespeares	20
Muskett arrowes	1000
Tampions	2100
Saltpeter	5 cwt
Brimaton	462lb
Flasks and tourchboxes for muskets	200
Fierworkes	1 barrell full

Write down two reasons why written sources from Tudor times like this one are
difficult to read:

1 _____

2 _____

What information does a written source such as this provide?

Name _____

Fact or opinion?

Tick the boxes to show which of these statements you think are fact and which are opinion.

	Fact	Opinion
Philip II was a coward.	☐	☐
Elizabeth was very brave.	☐	☐
Philip was a Catholic.	☐	☐
Elizabeth was a Protestant.	☐	☐
The English sailors were braver than the Spanish.	☐	☐
English ships were smaller than the Spanish galleons.	☐	☐
Sir Francis Drake fought the Armada.	☐	☐
The Duke of Medina Sidonia was in charge of the Armada.	☐	☐
It must have been good fun to be on a warship.	☐	☐
The Armada made England great.	☐	☐

Assessment sheet

Name _____

HISTORY STUDY KITS
THE TUDORS

I have used these sources to find out about the Spanish Armada:

I found out that:

I know more facts about the Armada than Will in the diary because:

Will would know more than me about:

How do we know?

Contents

How do we know?

Background information

The teachers' notes at the beginning of this *Study Kit* set out in detail what types of primary and secondary source material can be used to find out about life in Tudor England. They also indicate the problems involved with lack of evidence.

The Lesson plans and resource materials are intended to show how historical sources can be used at primary school level and how children can learn to identify the absence of evidence.

The Lesson plan in this section examines Will's diary and shows how it gives children a much broader perspective on the Tudor period and helps them to develop important historical concepts and understanding.

The diary format provides children with an opportunity to experience a particular genre of historical fiction so that they can use it as a model for their own creative writing.

What's true and how do we know?

Plymouth

The story is set in Plymouth at the time of the Armada. To find out about Plymouth in Tudor times, the authors of this pack spent several days there and traced records in the museum,

library and record office. They also talked with staff at the museum who have studied the history of Plymouth for many years.

They then visited Tudor sites in the area, in particular, the Elizabethan House in New Street, which unfortunately has since been closed to the public.

This is one of the few houses which have survived almost unaltered from the Tudor period and so it made a good base from which the story could start.

The street was not given the name New Street until the 18th century. Before then, it was probably called Grey Friars Street, which indicates that there may have been a friary nearby.

Evidence of New Street's Tudor origins can still be seen and, for those who live too far away to make a visit to New Street, illustrations are provided in this Study Kit.

In Tudor times, Plymouth was relatively prosperous and houses such as the Elizabethan House would have been built for merchants and sea captains near to the quayside where much of their business would be carried out.

Archaeological evidence shows that a new quay was built in 1572, although the present quay dates from the turn of the twentieth century.

However, questions have been raised about the name *Elizabethan House,* as details of the structure suggest it is more likely to have been built in the early seventeenth century.

The authors' investigations produced a collection of primary and secondary source material, building up a picture of what Plymouth looked like in 1587.

From this they have selected the material that is most useful and suitable for children at Key Stage 2.

Some of the information collected has been used as background for Will's diary and some has been used in the resource section of the Study Kit.

The rest of the information on life in Plymouth has been gleaned from more general evidence about life in Tudor towns. Reference has also been made to living

Plymouth's City Museum and Art Gallery is a good source of information on the history of the city at the time of the Armada.

conditions in the country. Town and country life was closely linked and this is shown several times in the diary — particularly in the description of the market.

Life on board ship

The life of the ordinary seaman in Tudor times has not been documented, so Will's daily routine has been drawn from what little information is known about life on board a small *bark* or boat.

It is not clear what a bark would have really looked like and, as with much of the shipping in Tudor times, we have to depend

The 'Armada portrait' of Elizabeth I is often used as evidence for the design of the ships involved in the conflict with the Armada.

on paintings, drawings and written source material, such as the famous Armada portrait. However, many of these pieces are not contemporary.

Written source material also needs to be treated with caution although we can make several good assumptions.

For example, when men such as Lord Howard were driven to write to several of the Queen's ministers about conditions for seamen, things must have been bad:

'Sickness and death begin to wonderfully grow among us. It is a most pitiful sight to see....how the men, having no place to go, die in the streets. I myself have come ashore to find them some lodging....It would grieve any man's heart to see them that have served so bravely to die so miserably.'
Howard to Burghley, August 1588

More seamen died from disease than died in battle.

The dangers of disease are also recorded in Will's diary (12 July):

'There is a lot of sickness on board the ships. Lord Howard's own fleet off Cattewater has fever aboard and Thomas told me that the soldiers have orders to kill anyone who tries to jump ship and run away. It must be awful for them.

One important source of information for life in Tudor England is the Tudor warship, the *Mary Rose*. This was one of Henry VIII's ships and it sank as it sailed out of Portsmouth harbour in 1545. The ship was lifted out of the water in 1982 and is now on display in Portsmouth.

More than 14,000 artefacts from the ship were found and these have provided valuable evidence not only about the daily life of sailors but also about life on land.

It is material such as this which helps to illustrate some of the key elements required by the history National Curriculum.

They are practical examples of the economic, technological and scientific elements of the Tudor era and they also provide visual sources for the social, cultural and aesthetic life of the period.

Political events

The main political event in the diary is the defeat of the Spanish Armada.

There is considerable source material for this but some of it needs to be used with caution, particularly the Victorian paintings which are easily accessible to primary children and are frequently used in reference books (see section on the Armada, page 168). Children need to be guided when using these pictures and taught how to interpret such source material.

The information in the diary relating directly to the events of the Armada is based on known fact.

Lord Howard was in charge of the English ships and the *Disdain,* Will's ship, did sail behind Howard's ship, the *Ark Royal*. There was a lot of sickness on board and there were orders to kill anyone who tried to leave the ships.

The *Disdain* did fire the first cannon shot at the Armada. Water and food supplies were low and Drake did capture a Spanish galleon called the *Rosario*.

The assumption has been made that ordinary seamen, like Thomas and Will, would have little understanding about the causes of the war with Spain (see the entry in Will's diary on 24 June).

Activity sheet G in this section asks children why they know more than Thomas does. This could be used as a basis for discussion about the children's knowledge of current events.

Some reference has been made to the fear of Spanish spies (6 April) and teachers with older children could explore this issue in relation to the persecution of Catholics that was taking place at this time.

A visit to a Tudor building which has priest holes would be helpful here.

Social relationships

This is perhaps one of the hardest aspects of history to examine.

Some artefacts exist to show the social and cultural aspects of people's lives but only written evidence exists to show the social relationships between people.

The diary uses this source material to show how Will's relationships with the adults around him differs from that which children today experience.

Some children may have had experience of older brothers and sisters being sent away from home to work but the majority will not. This can be explored through the diary as can the harsh regime on board ship.

The diary finishes when the Armada has left but Will's story can be continued in the classroom.

Having heard the diary read aloud, the children could recount events in the story and respond to questions about life in Tudor England. They could predict, speculate and hypothesise about what might happen to Will in the future.

The diary also gives the children some idea of the different points of view that people held at the time about the Armada. For example, they could discuss Will's point of view compared with that of his Aunt.

Dramatising events from the diary in small groups can also help the children to explore social relationships. They could even use the specialist historical language of the period.

In addition, a selection of historical fiction, from diaries to reference books, should be made available for the children so that they can read about events from as many different points of view as possible.

This will also help to develop the children's skills in using structural guiders, such as contents pages and glossaries. They will also become familiar with and be able to interpret chapter titles, headings, keys to symbols and abbreviations.

Finally, *Will's first battle* could be used to stimulate creative writing in which children can explore different characters' feelings and their relationships with others.

As they write, the children can build up a history word bank using many of the words included in the diary.

Additional spell checks could be done using a dictionary or a spell check facility on a word processor.

Working individually or in groups, the children could create extended texts, lay them out and illustrate them. Perhaps they could carry out a newspaper interview with Will after the Armada has left Plymouth.

The children can discuss how Will's relationship with the adults around him differs from their own.

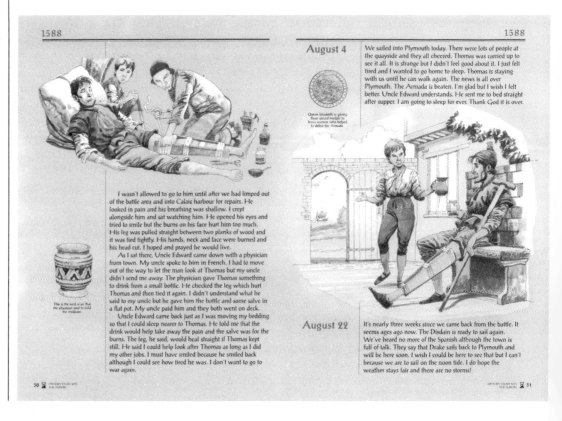

Lesson Plan : How do we know?

Objectives

Classroom based activities
1. Sequencing events in the diary.
2. Understanding of historical fiction in relation to history.
3. Developing concepts related to archaeology, bias, evidence, hypothesis.
4. Empathising with characters in the diary.
5. Examining historical sources from different points of view.
6. Skills in chronology.
7. Skill in interpreting historical fiction as a secondary source.

Homework
1. Skill in interpreting historical fiction as a secondary source.

Resources
Diary, reference books, tape recorder, video, computer.

Display
Children's own diaries. Photographs of children interviewing each other.

Content

Introduction
The diary can be read aloud to children in several sittings or read together as a class activity. Children should be able to:
1. recall and sequence events in the diary. This can be done through either written or pictorial work or by using activity sheet C.

Development
1. Children work in pairs – Child A is an interviewer for television, radio or a newspaper, preferably armed with a tape recorder, and Child B is Will. Child A interviews Child B for ten minutes about Will's part in the Spanish Armada. Both children can write up the interview for a newspaper article, video it for a television programme or edit the tape for a radio programme.

Extension activities
1. Look at what is known fact in the diary, using activity sheet B.
2. Write a diary from the viewpoint of someone else in the story – such as Will's aunt, Thomas or Will's mother. Children may need to use reference books to find out more information about town and country life.

Homework activities
1. Read another fictional story about the Tudors, such as *Under the Rose* by Alan Childs (Anglia), *Princes in the Pigpen* by J Thomas (Collins) or *Sir Francis Drake: His Daring Deeds* by Roy Gerrard (Gollancz).
2. Record any known facts mentioned in the story.

Assessment

AT 1, Level 1a – Sequence diary events. *
AT 1, Level 2b – Suggest reasons why Butcher did not want to fight the Spanish. *
AT 1, Level 2c – Identify differences between Will's life and their own. *
AT 1, Level 3b – Give reasons why men were dying on board ship before the Armada. **Level 3c** – Suggest why this sort of sickness did not affect men serving in the Royal or Merchant Navy during the last war.
AT 1, Level 4a – Recognise that the caution and fears expressed about going to war by Will's uncle and aunt are similar to those expressed today by many people.
AT 1, Level 4b – Show that there was more than one cause for and consequence of Will leaving home in Tavistock.
AT 1, Level 4c – Record different aspects of life in Plymouth in Tudor times.
AT 1, Level 6c – Record different views on the Spanish Armada.
AT 2, Level 1 – Be able to show that some of the events in the diary are true.
AT 2, Level 2 – Compare a description about the Spanish Armada in a reference book with Will's account.
AT 2, Level 3 – In the diary, distinguish between what is known to be true and what has been created.
AT 2, Level 4 – Show an awareness that the lack of source material means that very little is known about conditions on board ships such as the *Disdain*.
AT 2, Level 5 – Recognise that pictures such as that of Drake on the Hoe, and illustrations, are part of a myth-making process about events in history but are still useful source material.
AT 2, Level 6 – Show how Will's diary can be used as a secondary source, recognising that it must be interpreted according to Will's economic and social position.
AT 3, Level 1 – Describe what can be seen in one of the illustrations in the diary. *
AT 3, Level 2 – Recognise that historical fiction provides information about the past.
AT 3, Level 3 – Use illustrations of artefacts in the diary to find out more about life on board ship in Tudor times. Identify the use of such secondary source material.
AT 3, Level 4 – Use information from the diary, books and pictures to describe life in Plymouth at the time of the Armada.
AT 3, Level 5 – Discuss how historical fiction, eg Will's diary, can provide information/understanding about the past.
AT 3, Level 6 – Comment on the advantages and disadvantages of the diary and written historical sources – primary and secondary – in relation to life on board ship.

* Suitable for lower ability levels.

Fact sheet A

Name _____

Timeline from Will's first battle

1534
Henry VIII declares himself Supreme Head of the Church of England. This upsets the leaders
of many Catholic countries, particularly Spain.

1553
Mary Tudor marries Philip of Spain, ignoring the advice of her advisers who
warned the Queen that the marriage would be unpopular.

1559
After Mary dies, two events make the relationship between England and Spain even more difficult.
First, Philip of Spain asks Elizabeth I to marry him but she refuses. Secondly, Spanish ships are regularly
attacked and raided by English pirates and adventurers such as Sir Francis Drake and John Hawkins.

1579
Spain gives its support to a Catholic revolt in Ireland.

1584
The Spanish ambassador is expelled from England, accused of being
involved in a plot to overthrow Elizabeth I.

1585
To stop the English from helping the Dutch protestants in their revolt against Spain,
the Spanish seize some English ships while they are in port.

1586
Francis Drake raids land in the West Indies that is owned by the Spanish. It becomes clear
that Elizabeth has given Drake money for his expedition. Philip gets ready to attack
England with a fleet of ships.

1587
Drake destroys this Spanish fleet at Cadiz.

1588

February
The English fleet gathers at Plymouth, headed
by Lord Howard.

May
The Spanish Armada sets sail under the leadership of
the Duke of Medina Sidonia.

August
The Armada is defeated in an eight-hour battle near
Gravelines and retreats via Scotland and Ireland
where it is hit by storms.

Name _____

Who's who?

Use Will's diary to find pictures of the people named below. Draw your own pictures of each person in the space provided.

Will	Will's aunt	Sir Francis Drake
Lord Howard	Uncle Edward	Elizabeth I

Activity sheet B

Name _____

Fact or fiction?

When you have read Will's diary, put a tick in
the box to show which of the following
statements you think are true or false.

	True	False	Don't know
Will Martin was a boy who lived in Tudor times and fought in the Armada.	☐	☐	☐
Men on the *Disdain* were brave.	☐	☐	☐
The house in the diary is real.	☐	☐	☐
Sailors drank ale rather than water.	☐	☐	☐
Disease killed more sailors than the Spanish did.	☐	☐	☐
Sir Francis Drake visited the house in New Street.	☐	☐	☐
People stood up during church services.	☐	☐	☐
The *Disdain* was a large naval warship.	☐	☐	☐
Plymouth is in Devon.	☐	☐	☐
Will went back to live with his family on the farm.	☐	☐	☐

Name _____

Sequencing

Here are six extracts from Will's diary. When
you have read the diary, cut up the extracts
and put them in the right order.

We finally got out of
harbour and headed due
south with Lord
Howard's fleet. When we
first saw the mighty
Spanish Armada it filled us
with awe. There were
hundreds of ships all close
together in the shape of a
huge crescent moon. The
largest galleons were
protecting the smaller
ships.

The house is in chaos
today. Cook told me that
the great Sir Francis
Drake was to visit Uncle
Edward and stay to
supper. I had to help clean
the house from attic to
cellar and cook spent ages
making the supper. I was
really excited about seeing
him. He is so famous.

There was a splendid feast
waiting for us when we
got back to Plymouth.
Thomas came and we all
got presents. Uncle
Edward gave me a real
dagger with jewels in the
horn handle. He said he
took it from a Spanish
soldier at Cadiz and it is
mine now.

I have been terribly sick
for four days now and no
one helped me - not even
Uncle Edward! They just
left me to lie on the deck
with a sack over me and a
bucket by my side to be
sick into. It started soon
after we had sailed out of
the Sound and the ship
started pitching and rolling
on the waves.

We sailed into Plymouth
today. There were lots of
people at the quayside
and they all cheered,
Thomas was carried up to
see it all. It is strange but I
didn't feel good about it. I
just felt tired and I
wanted to go home to
sleep. Thomas is staying
with us until he can walk
again. The news is all over
Plymouth. The Armada is
beaten.

This afternoon I was sent
to help the cook gut the
fish and boil it! It's not
fair! I might just as well
be back at Plymouth
working in the kitchen.
I'll never get to be a
ship's master if all I do is
wash down the decks and
cook!

Choose two or three extracts then illustrate them on a separate sheet of paper.

Activity sheet D

Name _____

What is wrong?

Put a circle around five artefacts that would not have been here in Tudor times.

Explain why you have circled each object.

Name _____

Mystery objects

Use Will's diary to find out more about these artefacts.

1

2

3

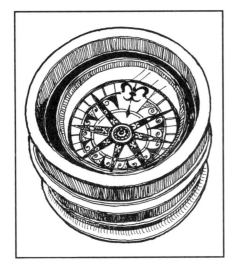

4

Picture 1 is _____

Picture 2 is _____

Picture 3 is _____

Picture 4 is _____

Activity sheet F

Name _____

Causes of the battle with the Spanish Armada

On 24 June, Will asked Thomas why the Spanish wanted to attack the English. Thomas said that he did not really understand why.

Use the diary and reference books to answer Will's question.

Why do you know more than Thomas?

Name _____

Using written sources: Baptisms, July 1588

These are the names of children baptised in St Andrew's Church in Plymouth in July 1588.

Cristian	d of Nicolas Saywell
Grace	d of George Mules
Jone	d of Francs Bass
John	s of John Rawe
Richard	s of Gregory Holman
Mighel	s of Pancras Webber
John	s of Henry Cowlyn
Peeter	s of John Yemans
Willm	s of Erasmus Yelsey
Florence and Jone	ds of Richard Moone
Thomason	d of Nic Rowse
Francis	d of William Greepe
Jone	d of John Edwardes
John	s of Hugh Smythe
John	s of Thomas Ostler
Willm	s of Willm Hobbes
Elizebeth	d of James Ashely
Judeth	d of John Tracy
Elinir	d of Abraham Howell
Georg	s of Andrew Lange
Judeth	d of Robert Forde

The burial register for July 1588 tells us that 69 people were buried at the church including:

Cristian	d of Nic Saywell
Katheren	w of Nic Saywell
Peeter	s of John Yeman
Jone	d of John Edwardes

How many of the children baptised in July lived until August? Take care, w stands for wife.

How many children were baptised in July 1588?

_____

How many girls were baptised?

_____

How many boys were baptised?

_____

What were the twins called?

_____

Assessment sheet

Name _____

I have read Will's diary and in it I have seen the following photographs of Tudor artefacts:

I have read Will's diary and in it I have seen the following illustrations:

Will's diary gives us evidence about:

I have used the following reference books to find out more about the Armada: